普通高等学校"十四五"规划英语专业数字化精品系列教材

- 2020年度北京市教育委员会社科计划一般项目"基于OBE理念的对话型信息化大学英语课堂教学模式的构建与实践(SM202010005013)"成果
- 2020年度北京工业大学教育教学研究课题"'网络+课堂+实践'三位一体的'外语+中国文化'课程思政育人体系建设与实践(ER2020B065)"成果
- 2021年度北京工业大学"三全育人"教师团队一般培育项目"'外语教学+中国价值':高校外语课程思政育人体系建设"成果
- 2020年度北京工业大学"课程思政"示范课程培育项目"大学英语(综合)"成果
- 2021年度北京工业大学研究生"课程思政"示范课程培育项目"普通语言学"成果

# 中国文化简明英语教程

## Concise English Course on Chinese Culture

主　编　邹丽玲
副主编　王惠敏
编　者　(以姓氏笔画为序)
　　　　王晓利　刘昭仪　刘倩
　　　　刘慧灵　陈平　严璐
　　　　胡文婷

华中科技大学出版社
http://www.hustp.com
中国·武汉

图书在版编目(CIP)数据

中国文化简明英语教程/邹丽玲主编. —武汉:华中科技大学出版社,2021.9
ISBN 978-7-5680-7543-5

Ⅰ.①中… Ⅱ.①邹… Ⅲ.①中华文化-英语-阅读教学-教材 Ⅳ.①K203

中国版本图书馆 CIP 数据核字(2021)第 188111 号

中国文化简明英语教程　　　　　　　　　　　　　　　　　　邹丽玲　主编
Zhongguo Wenhua Jianming Yingyu Jiaocheng

策划编辑:周晓方　宋　焱
责任编辑:江旭玉
封面设计:廖亚萍
责任校对:张汇娟
责任监印:周治超

出版发行:华中科技大学出版社(中国·武汉)　　电话:(027)81321913
　　　　　武汉市东湖新技术开发区华工科技园　　邮编:430223
录　　排:华中科技大学出版社美编室
印　　刷:武汉科源印刷设计有限公司
开　　本:787mm×1092mm　1/16
印　　张:7.5　插页:1
字　　数:177 千字
版　　次:2021 年 9 月第 1 版第 1 次印刷
定　　价:28.00 元

本书若有印装质量问题,请向出版社营销中心调换
全国免费服务热线:400-6679-118　竭诚为您服务
版权所有　侵权必究

# 前言
## Preface

《中国文化简明英语教程》以阅读文章的形式介绍中国的新发展、新面貌,每个主题包括两篇文章,每篇文章涉及不同类型的练习题,涵盖语言知识、中国文化翻译等内容,帮助学生在阅读的过程中提高英语水平,夯实语言基础,拓展中国文化知识。本书旨在通过价值引领,帮助学生了解中国的新发展,提高语言应用能力及用英语讲述中国故事的能力,从而让学生坚定中国立场、培养文化自信。

本书的主要特点有三点:其一,内容编排兼具时效性和科学性,文章主要节选自中国国际电视台(英文简称 CGTN,中文别称中国环球电视网)等主流媒体中的最新英语语料,涵盖代表中国新发展的主要内容和当前的热点话题;其二,本书的设计兼具启发性和思辨性,在结构编排上从易到难,强调多样性和评价的多维度,避免单一类型的材料、题目贯彻始终,做到因材施教;其三,本书的内容重在提升学生的语言能力,贵在强化思政教育。文章选材以及编排的练习题处处体现培养学生家国情怀、责任担当、文化自信的价值引领目标。

本教程由8个单元组成:第1单元介绍中国新科技;第2单元介绍中国新交通;第3单元介绍中国新建筑;第4单元介绍中国新商务;第5单元介绍中国新生活;第6单元介绍中国新环境;第7单元介绍中国新教育;第8单元介绍中国新经济。每个单元有两篇文章,每篇文章配有不同类型的习题。习题部分包括生词练习、句子练习、篇章理解、句子翻译、段落翻译、主题讨论等。此外,每篇文章配备单词和长难句的讲解,学生可以在教师的指导下学习语言知识,也可自主学习。

具体编写分工如下:刘昭仪负责第1单元;王惠敏负责第2单元;王晓利负责第3单元;邹丽玲、刘慧灵负责第4单元;陈平负责第5单元;严璐负责第6单元;胡文婷负责第7单元;刘倩负责第8单元。

本教材具有较强的针对性和实用性,配有阅读测试材料,适合英语专业、非英语专业的本科生、研究生阅读类英语课程使用,也适合具有一定英语基础的学习者自主提高阅读能力使用。在教材编写过程中,我们得到了华中科技大学出版社的大力支持,在此深表感谢。敬请各位同仁对本教材存在的不足予以批评指正。

编　者
2021 年 4 月

# 目录
## Contents

**Unit 1　China's New Technology** ········································· (1)
　Text A　A "Golden Phoenix" Takes off ······························ (1)
　Text B　BeiDou's Completion Will Wind up the Monopoly Era of
　　　　　GPS ······················································· (8)

**Unit 2　China's New Transportation** ······································ (15)
　Text A　China's Growing Strength in Transport ····················· (15)
　Text B　CRH380A High Speed Train ··································· (22)

**Unit 3　China's New Architecture** ······································· (29)
　Text A　Wuhan's Huoshenshan Hospital: A Symbol of Chinese Spirit ······ (29)
　Text B　Hong Kong-Zhuhai-Macao Bridge: A Megaproject Full of
　　　　　Chinese Wisdom ············································ (37)

**Unit 4　China's New Commerce** ·········································· (44)
　Text A　What It's Like to Live in a Cashless Society ················ (44)
　Text B　Xiabuxiabu ··················································· (50)

**Unit 5　China's New Life** ·············································· (56)
　Text A　China's "Gen Z":
　　　　　Patriotic and No Longer Looking up to the West ············· (56)
　Text B　Twenty-Five Years of Gender Equality in China ············· (62)

1

**Unit 6　China's New Environment** ·········································· (67)

　　Text A　Moving to a Green Economy ································· (67)

　　Text B　Gaming the System ············································· (74)

**Unit 7　China's New Education** ············································· (80)

　　Text A　New Era of Education in China ···························· (80)

　　Text B　The COVID-19 Pandemic Has Changed Education Forever ······· (90)

**Unit 8　China's New Economy** ············································· (100)

　　Text A　China's Growth Gives Confidence to World Economy ············ (100)

　　Text B　Country Roads Lead to Success ····························· (106)

**参考文献** ··············································································· (115)

# Unit 1
# China's New Technology

## Text A   A "Golden Phoenix" Takes off

Located in southern Beijing's Daxing District, the Beijing Daxing International Airport (BDIA) is expected to become north China's air travel hub. Calling the airport a "perfect combination of Chinese culture and modern architecture", He Lifeng, the head of the National Development and Reform Commission, said it demonstrates the great achievements China has made in its social and economic development and infrastructure construction during the 70 years since its founding.

Straddling Beijing's Daxing District and Guangyang District of Langfang in Hebei Province, BDIA is located at the junction of Beijing, Tianjin and Hebei. Thanks to a comprehensive "five vertical and two horizontal" transportation network, which integrates the highway, intercity railway, high-speed railway and subways with the airport as the center, passengers can choose the right mode of transportation according to their travel plans and preferences. The airport's location at the center of intercity transportation networks will make it easily accessible, while it is anticipated that it will also promote the region's integrated development.

Under construction since 2015, BDIA was listed as the first of the "seven wonders of the modern world near completion" by the UK-based newspaper *The Guardian* that year. The new airport's shape reveals its designers' virtuosity and understanding of traditional Chinese culture. In China, the legendary phoenix epitomizes beauty and auspiciousness. Designed with six piers radiating from the heart of the terminal, BDIA embodies the traditional Chinese architectural principle of organizing interconnected spaces around a central courtyard.

BDIA is not just about the eye-catching architecture, the unprecedented terminal area, and the sophisticated design. Multiple cutting-edge technologies in the new airport will make traveling a breeze. So what kinds of intelligent services can we expect from the red "starfish"?

## Intelligent Robotic Parking System

Tired of finding parking at the airport? It's time to say goodbye to that nightmare.

The BDIA is expected to be the first in the country to implement a trial run of an automated parking system that will reduce the parking time to within one minute. Drivers only need to park their cars on a platform, and robots will lift the cars and transport them to empty spots.

"The system is equipped with 132 parking spaces, 6 parking rooms and 8 robots," said Ba Gen, the chief engineer of the BDIA's IT department. "The environment-friendly robots can lift up to 3.5 metric tons," Ba added. "They produce zero emissions and can work for up to six hours on a single charge, before automatically making their way to their charging station."

"Robots are taught to dodge obstacles in real time, and avoid getting dents or scratches from parking lot mishaps," the engineer explained. When customers want to collect their cars, they just need to scan their parking tickets or enter their plate numbers using a terminal, which tells them where to go to collect their cars. It takes less than two minutes for the cars to be delivered, cited *Asia Times*.

## Futuristic Boarding Experience

Apart from the intelligent parking system, high-tech solutions can be seen everywhere.

Facial recognition technology aiming to speed up the security check and boarding processes has finished its trial run recently. Passengers are expected to have a paperless self-service experience from the terminal entrance to their boarding gate. According to the Civil Aviation Administration of China, self-service check-in kiosks will have 86 percent coverage at the new Beijing airport.

The radio-frequency identification (RFID) baggage tracking system enables passengers and airport staff to check baggage status and location in a timely manner. Chips on the RFID tag, which are attached to the items you want to track, can be read by the overhead doorway scanners as they pass through checkpoints.

The Wi-Fi indoor location technology provided by Huawei can help airport operators rapidly calculate passenger traffic and accordingly open or close the security check channels to improve operation efficiency.

## Next-generation Robots in the Airport

In the terminal of the new airport, 10 virtual interactive kiosks and just as many humanoid robots are ready to answer questions from passengers.

"These interactive kiosks are the upgraded version of the previous speech-recognizing robots. Based on 3D Portrait technology, the animated virtual assistant generated in the kiosk is able to have life-like conversations with passengers," said the project manager of BDIA's information management department.

"Besides basic information inquiry services, they are also equipped with automatic positioning functions. As long as passengers are in need, the kiosks will optimize for the best routes, directing them to their destinations," he added. What's more, sensor-embedded humanoid robots are able to announce breaking news and major events.

"As a major landmark project in the capital, the new airport's operation plays a significant role in improving the international competitiveness of China's civil aviation (industry), better supporting the country's opening to the outside world, decentralizing Beijing's non-capital functions, and promoting coordinated development of the Beijing-Tianjin-Hebei region," said Chinese Vice Premier Han Zheng.

Han said he hopes the airport can be a new benchmark for the construction and operation of an international aviation hub, and it will serve as a world-class gateway to China. The new airport, together with Beijing Capital International Airport, should form part of a modern international aviation hub that connects the whole world. The airport is also expected to proactively promote reform and innovation in the Beijing-Tianjin-Hebei region, as well as the development of the Xiongan New Area.

**Source:**

[1] https://news.cgtn.com/news/2019-06-30/Here-are-the-futuristic-technologies-in-the-new-Beijing-airport-HWi36zaeg8/index.html.

[2] https://news.cgtn.com/news/2019-09-25/President-Xi-announces-opening-of-new-Beijing-airport-KgPlEZB3Z6/index.html.

[3] https://news.cgtn.com/news/2019-10-25/Beijing-Daxing-International-Airport-30-days-in-L4V4eaONLa/index.html.

# Language Focus

## Ⅰ. Useful Expressions

(1) auspiciousness　　　　　　　n. 吉兆;吉祥
(2) cutting-edge　　　　　　　　adj. 领先的,最新的;先进的,尖端的
(3) dodge　　　　　　　　　　　v. 躲开;迅速让开
(4) environment-friendly　　　　adj. 有利于环境的;环保型的
(5) epitomize　　　　　　　　　v. 摘要;概括
(6) eye-catching　　　　　　　　adj. 引人注目的;耀眼的;显著的
(7) horizontal　　　　　　　　　adj. 水平的;地平线的
(8) hub　　　　　　　　　　　　n. 中心
(9) kiosk　　　　　　　　　　　n. 凉亭;公用电话亭;报摊
(10) legendary　　　　　　　　　adj. 传说的,传奇的
(11) phoenix　　　　　　　　　　n. 凤凰
(12) plate number　　　　　　　n. 车牌
(13) trial run　　　　　　　　　n. 初步试验,试行
(14) vertical　　　　　　　　　adj. 垂直的,直立的
(15) virtuosity　　　　　　　　　n. 精湛技巧,高超技艺

## Ⅱ. Difficult Sentence

Thanks to a comprehensive "five vertical and two horizontal" transportation network, which integrates the highway, intercity railway, high-speed railway and subways with the airport as the center, passengers can choose the right mode of transportation according to their travel plans and preferences.

**翻译**:多亏了以机场为中心,公路、城际铁路、高速铁路、地铁为一体的"五纵两横"综合交通网络,乘客们可以根据自己的出行计划和喜好选择合适的交通方式。

**分析**:Thanks to 为复合介词,后接名词,在句中作原因状语,相当于 because of,可翻译为"多亏""由于"。跟在其后的为 which 引导的非限制性定语从句,对"五纵两横"综合交通网络进行解释说明。后面是主句,该句主语为 passengers,主句中 according to 意为"根据",为复合介词,后多接名词。

该句子说明了综合交通网络的便捷性以及出行方式的多样性,为人们提供了更多选择。

# Exercises

## Ⅰ. Reading and Understanding

**Decide whether the statements are true or false.**

(1) Located between Beijing and Langfang, Hebei Province, which is far from city center, it can be quite a difficult way for passengers to get to the new airport.

(2) Evolved from principles within traditional Chinese architecture, this phoenix-shaped airport also features some state-of-the-art technologies.

(3) When customers want to collect their cars, the robot in the parking system will tell them where to go to collect their cars.

(4) Passengers can have their faces scanned to check in their luggage, clear security and board the aircraft, which dispenses with showing an ID, holding tickets or scanning QR codes.

(5) Passengers can interact with the customer-service robots to ask for directions, and the robot will take the passengers to their destinations.

## II. Dealing with Unfamiliar Words

### 1. Match the words in the left with their definitions.

(1) infrastructure     a. an open space that is completely or partly surrounded by buildings

(2) virtuosity     b. something that is used as a standard by which other things can be judged or measured

(3) courtyard     c. having a human shape and human qualities

(4) humanoid     d. the basic systems and structures that a country or organization needs in order to work properly, for example, roads, railways, banks, etc.

(5) benchmark     e. a very high degree of skill in performing

### 2. Word Study

Below are some commonly occurring affixes. Study their meanings and then do the exercises that follow.

| Affix | Meaning | Example |
| --- | --- | --- |
| inter- | between, among | intercity, interconnected |
| mis- | bad, wrong | mishap |
| avi- | bird | aviation |
| de- | down, away | decentralize, decline |
| pro- | forward, forth | proactive, prolong |

Following is a list of words containing the affixes introduced in this text. Definitions of these words appear on the right. Put the letter of the appropriate definition next to each word.

(1) proponent     a. to say publicly or officially that something important is true or exists

(2) interrupt            b. an incorrect or mistaken understanding of something

(3) misnomer             c. someone who supports something or persuades people to do something

(4) proclaim             d. come between others in time; interfere so as to prevent something or change the result

(5) debar                e. to stop someone from continuing what they are saying or doing by suddenly speaking to them, making a noise, etc.

(6) aviator              f. to officially prevent someone from doing something

(7) misconstruction      g. a pilot

(8) aviary               h. a wrong or unsuitable name

(9) intervene            i. to be slowly destroyed by a natural chemical process, or to make something do this

(10) decay               j. an incorrect or mistaken understanding of something

## III. Developing Critical Thinking

**Work in pairs and discuss the questions.**

(1) Do you think technology will replace service jobs in emerging markets? Why?

(2) What do you think are the significance and influence of the construction of BDIA?

扫码看答案

# Text B  BeiDou's Completion Will Wind up the Monopoly Era of GPS

With the launch of the final satellite in the BeiDou Navigation Satellite System (BDS) around the corner, China will be completing the installation of the third generation of the network. This marks one of the most significant milestones in China's technological journey in space utilization. The independent development and operation of the system took 20 years, over 100,000 experts and more than 300 domestic institutes and enterprises to mature and set out on the path of becoming the most advanced navigational facility ever. While providing all-weather and accurate positioning services, BDS has already come to surpass many capabilities of the U.S.-launched Global Positioning System (GPS)—a much older technological feat.

## BDS's Biggest Strength Is Its Accuracy

A scrutinous look at the superiority of BDS reveals that accuracy is its biggest strength. With decimeter-level dynamic positioning and centimeter-level static positioning, it can provide location services down to the accuracy of 10 cm in the Asia-Pacific region. The GPS, meanwhile, has the limitation of rendering a maximum of 30 cm of accuracy. This is because BeiDou uses much higher bandwidth under the concept of Precise Point Positioning function provided by its three geostationary Earth orbit satellites.

The higher accuracy of BDS has introduced new concepts in global positioning usage. Precision at the sub-meter level allows the technology's application in wearable devices like children's watches and bracelets for the elderly. As its product ecosystem will continue to sprout, it will be possible to mass manufacture inexpensive and small-sized tracking devices. Losing sight of anything or anyone loved will then be a thing of the past.

## BDS Will Be on E-commerce

A greater impact would be on e-commerce. The cheaper and smaller BeiDou tracking devices will be embedded in packages, allowing sellers and buyers to actively follow their delivery status and make further commitments to clients with confidence. China's existing leadership in e-commerce will, therefore, be strengthened, while simultaneously assisting other stakeholders in improving their revenues.

## The Function of the Text Messaging that the GPS Does Not Have

Then there is BeiDou's advantage of the text messaging that the GPS does not have. Presently, we are dependent on cell phones to request for help in cases of emergency. Due to the drawback of limited coverage in remote areas, people shift to the relatively expensive satellite phones.

But with the messaging feature of BeiDou, a new concept of connected mobility is emerging. Thousands of fishing boats in China have already installed BDS, which enables them to communicate in times of distress. The same is true for outdoor sportspeople who are often outside of cell phone coverage in mountains and remain vulnerable to disaster situations. As 5G is changing the way we connect in urban areas, text messaging through BeiDou is likewise changing the way people connect in the remotest of areas.

## The Win-win Aspiration of BDS

BDS, being a Chinese system, has another inherent Chinese characteristic: the win-win aspiration. Under this endeavor, China is promoting compatibility with other navigation systems. Traditionally, western technologies have attempted to maintain their monopoly for commercial and other reasons. BDS instead aims to become a global good so that all people around the world can benefit.

For this purpose, China has established a coordination mechanism with the U.S. which ensures signal interoperability. In addition to that, China and the EU are cooperating in frequency coordination. But the most extensive collaboration that BDS has is with Russia's GLONASS, abbreviated from Global Navigation Satellite System. BDS and GLONASS have been cooperating since 2018 when an agreement was signed between the two sides to promote navigational equipment making use of both the systems. With monitoring stations installed in the two countries, correcting navigation signals will improve performance and allow operators to seamlessly switch from one network to the other. Moreover, users will benefit from GLONASS's coverage in high-altitude areas and BeiDou's coverage in low-altitude areas.

Today's communication and transportation are increasingly becoming sophisticated. And as the world is equally becoming dependent on them to efficiently deliver products and services, reliance on GPS as the single source of navigational guidance was becoming riskier.

### BDS Provides the World an Alternative

BDS has ultimately provided the world an alternative. With a single player or with the monopoly of a single player in the market, development and innovation almost becomes non-existent. The completion of BDS is now giving users an additional option for comparison. They can either opt for the better one or make use of the combination of both.

### BDS Will Unleash a New Era in Global Navigation and Positioning

From a technical perspective, BDS has several advantages over GPS. As its satellites use fewer orbit planes, it is far easier to maintain. It has more satellites than GPS, GLONASS or the European Galileo Satellite Navigation System. And lastly, its performance in covered settings is also superior, thereby giving it higher accuracy indoors, underground and underwater.

All things considered, the completion of the BDS network will unleash a new era in global navigation and positioning. With its improved features, it has brought cutting edge, yet affordable facilities that will bolster economic activity and augment the efficiency of supply chains. Chinese technology has come of age. While breaking the monopoly of traditional entities, it is making an invaluable contribution to the global scientific progress.

Source:

http://www.bjreview.com/China/202006/t20200624_800211574.html.

# Language Focus

## Ⅰ. Useful Expressions

(1) all-weather　　　　　　*adj.* 全天候的;适应各种气候的

(2) around the corner　　　*adv.* 即将来临

(3) bandwidth　　　　　　*n.* 带宽;频带宽度

(4) bracelet　　　　　　　*n.* 手镯;手链

(5) ecosystem　　　　　　*n.* 生态系统

(6) opt for　　　　　　　 *v.* 选择

(7) scrutinous　　　　　　*adj.* 好刨根问底的;仔细查看的

(8) stakeholders　　　　　*n.* 利益相关者

(9) superiority　　　　　　*n.* 优越,优势;优越性

(10) supply chains　　　　 *n.* 供应链

## Ⅱ. Difficult Sentence

With its improved features, it has brought cutting edge, yet affordable facilities that will bolster economic activity and augment the efficiency of supply chains.

**翻译**:随着其功能的改进,它带来了尖端的,但负担得起的设施,这将促进经济活动,提高供应链的效率。

**分析**:With 后的内容作伴随状语。yet 用作连词,与 but 一样主要用于转折,意为"但是"。cutting edge, yet affordable 作 facilities 的定语,后为 that 引导的定语从句,说明设施的作用。

 # Exercises

## Ⅰ. Reading and Understanding

**Decide whether the statements are true or false.**

(1) Due to its sub-meter level positioning accuracy, BDS has already applied to

mass manufacture inexpensive and small-sized tracking devices, children's watches and the elderly's bracelets, for example.

(2) BDS will see fast adoption by China's modern logistics field.

(3) High precision positioning is a feature of BDS that GPS cannot do.

(4) Fishermen can send text messages via BeiDou satellites on the sea when there is no cellular signal.

(5) China has made effort to develop Beidou satellite navigation system to serve the whole world.

## II. Dealing with Unfamiliar Words

### 1. Match the words in the left with their definitions.

(1) navigation     a. to suddenly let a strong force, feeling, etc have its full effect

(2) orbit     b. the science or job of planning which way you need to go when you are travelling from one place to another

(3) unleash     c. to help someone to feel better and more positive

(4) bolster     d. to travel in a curved path around a much larger object such as the Earth, the Sun, etc.

(5) augment     e. to increase the value, amount, effectiveness etc. of something

### 2. Word Study

Below are some commonly occurring affixes. Study their meanings and then do the exercises that follow.

| Affix | Meaning | Example |
| --- | --- | --- |
| sur- | over, beyond | surpass |
| centi- | one hundredth | centimeter |
| mono- | one | monopoly |

| deci- | one tenth | decimeter |
| soph- | wise, wisdom | sophisticate |

Following is a list of words containing the affixes introduced in this unit. Definitions of these words appear on the right. Put the letter of the appropriate definition next to each word.

(1) decimate      a. when a person or animal has a sexual relationship with only one partner

(2) centipede      b. the study of nature and meaning of existence, truth, good and evil, etc.

(3) monogamy      c. to destroy a large part of something

(4) sophistry      d. a small creature like a worm with a lot of very small legs

(5) monogram      e. someone who is 100 years old or older

(6) centenarian      f. a fraction (a number less than 1) that is shown as a full stop followed by the number of tenths

(7) decimal      g. a design that is made using the first letters of someone's names and is put on pieces of clothing or other possessions

(8) surface      h. the clever use of reasons or explanations that seem correct but are really false, in order to deceive people

(9) surcharge      i. money that you have to pay in addition to the basic price of something

(10) philosophy      j. the outside or top layer of something

## Ⅲ. Translating the Paragraph into English

合作共赢是北斗的抱负,造福人类是北斗的责任。和平利用空间,开展深入的国际合作与交流,是我国的一贯立场。北斗系统为全球导航系统的发展注入了新思路、新理念和新动力。它不仅为全球社会经济发展、和平利用外空以及参与联合国国际空间合作做出巨大贡献,还为世界各国高等院校和科研机构提供了联合研发成果、产业合作和教育培训的机会。近年来,北斗系统服务水平不断提高,积极参与国际事务,履行国际义务,为多个国际组织提供服务。北斗系统必将为增进人类福祉、推动构建人类命运共同体发挥越来越重要的作用。

## Ⅳ. Developing Critical Thinking

**Work in pairs and discuss the questions.**

(1) Before the launch of BDS, only the U.S. and Russia possessed mature and self-developed satellite navigation systems, and GPS is open to the world free of charge. Why would China have to develop its own navigation system?

(2) What do you think of the influence of BDS? How does it change our lives?

扫码看答案

# Unit 2
# China's New Transportation

## Text A  China's Growing Strength in Transport

In the new era, China is accelerating the high-quality development of its transport industry—it is seeing consistent progress in infrastructure construction, marked improvements in transport capacity, quality and efficiency, stronger technological support, greater accessibility and convenience, and more efficient freight transport. China is building up its strength in transport.

China has taken advantage of a key window of opportunity to optimize the configuration of transport infrastructure and build it into a comprehensive network. The country has advanced supply-side structural reform in transport by bringing into service a group of passenger and freight hubs. The scale, quality and coverage of the comprehensive transport network have been significantly increased.

### Forming a Basic Network for Comprehensive Transport Infrastructure

By the end of 2019, China had a total of 139,000 km of rail track, of which high-speed lines represented 35,000 km, and a total of more than 5 million km of highways, of which expressways represented 150,000 km. The country had 23,000 operative berths, including 2,520 berths of 10,000-tonne-class or above, and 127,000 km of navigable inland waterways. There were 238 certified civil airports throughout the country. The long-distance oil and gas pipelines totaled 156,000 km with better connections achieved. The total network length of postal and express delivery services approximated 41 million km; every township had a post office and every village was provided with postal services. A comprehensive and multidimensional transport network has been put in place to give strong support to the sustained, rapid and healthy development of society and the economy.

## Connecting the Main Transport Corridors

The main transport corridors will be further expanded and connected to ensure China's territorial and energy security, and strengthen economic and political connections between regions. The state has devised ten vertical and ten horizontal transport corridors. Economic belts and city clusters are thriving along the transport corridors between Beijing and Shanghai, between Beijing and Guangzhou, along the Yangtze River and the coastlines, and near the ports in the Yangtze River Delta and Pearl River Delta and along the Bohai Sea Rim. They are becoming the most economically dynamic and populous areas in the country. Two thirds of the cities and 80 percent of the GDP of the Yangtze River Delta are concentrated along the high-speed transport corridors between Shanghai and Nanjing, and between Shanghai and Hangzhou. A rapid intercity transport network featuring high-speed railways, intercity railways and high-grade highways has been put in place in the Guangdong-Hong Kong-Macao Greater Bay Area.

A trunk network of gas pipelines is improving with the capacity to transmit gas from west to east China, from Sichuan to east China and from Shaanxi to Beijing, and to bring gas from offshore. Coal logistics corridors are better configured, and a railway corridor for energy transport running across the country has taken shape. The main logistics corridors for grain have been connected, and the container volumes of unprocessed grain, bulk grain and refined grain have increased significantly, along with improved efficiency in grain logistics. Flow of people and goods is more convenient between regions. An open and comprehensive transport network that crosses the whole country and connects with the world has taken shape.

## Building Integrated Transport Hubs

By giving full play to the hub economy and actively fostering new drivers of growth, China has promoted the integration of transport, logistics, and information with society and the economy. Considering the national urban configuration, the country has built international transport hubs in Beijing, Shanghai and Guangzhou, and created more transport hubs at national and regional levels. Highlighting the need for integrated transport terminals, a group of such projects have been completed, such as the Beijing Daxing and Shanghai Hongqiao hubs, integrating airport transport seamlessly with high-speed and standard rail, and urban passenger transport.

The configuration of freight terminals and logistics parks has been optimized for multimodal and multilevel transport. A number of modern logistics hubs, such as Yangshan Port in Shanghai and the railway inland port in Zhengzhou, have helped to improve the transshipment capacity, enhance multimodal transport, and create a comprehensive transport system. The integration of various transport methods at these hubs provides strong support for optimizing the economic structure and modernizing the economic system.

## Strengthening Systematic Planning for Urban Transport Infrastructure

By the end of 2019, the total length of urban roads across the country was 459,000 km, the road area per capita 17.36 sq. m, the road network density in the urban built-up areas was 6.65 km/sq. km and the road area ratio 13.19 percent. The government has strengthened planning for a comprehensive urban transport network and improved effective transport connections between cities and neighboring areas.

With a concept of "narrower roads and a denser network", China has built an urban road network featuring a reasonable composition of expressways, arterial roads, sub-arterial roads and branch roads friendly to green travel. The transport authorities have improved road space allocation to fully ensure the needs of green travel and regulated the provision of traffic safety and management facilities. The country has carried out campaigns to clear up sidewalks and build bike paths to improve the environment for green travel.

**Source:**
http://english.scio.gov.cn/whitepapers/2020-12/22/content_77040131_4.htm.

# Language Focus

## Ⅰ. Useful Expressions

(1) accelerate     v. 使……加快；使……增速
(2) accessibility     n. 易接近；可以得到
(3) allocate     v. 分配；拨出
(4) arterial roads     公路干线；(城市)主干路
(5) berth     n. 停泊处，泊位
(6) bulk grain     散粮；散装谷物
(7) configuration     n. 配置；结构
(8) feature     v. 以……为特色；特写
(9) foster     v. 促进；抚育
(10) infrastructure construction     基础设施；基础设施建设
(11) refined grain     细粮；精制谷物
(12) trunk     adj. 干线的；躯干的

## Ⅱ. Difficult Sentences

(1) By the end of 2019, China had a total of 139,000 km of rail track, of which high-speed lines represented 35,000 km, and a total of more than 5 million km of highways, of which expressways represented 150,000 km.

**翻译**：截至2019年底，全国铁路营业里程达到13.9万公里，其中高速铁路营业里程为3.5万公里；全国公路里程超过500万公里，其中高速公路里程15万公里。

**分析**：该句是由and连接的并列句。在and之前的分句中，句子主语是China，谓语是had，宾语是rail track，其中of which引导非限定性定语从句，对先行词rail track进行补充、说明，进一步明确在所有铁路中高速铁路的长度。与之类似，在and之后的分句中，句子主语是China，谓语是had，宾语是highways，其中of which引导非限定性定语从句，对先行词highways进行补充、说明，进一步明确在所有公路中高速公路的长度。

(2) A rapid intercity transport network featuring high-speed railways, intercity railways and high-grade highways has been put in place in the Guangdong-Hong Kong-Macao Greater Bay Area.

翻译:粤港澳大湾区形成了以高速铁路、城际铁路和高等级公路为主体的城际快速交通网络。

分析:该句为被动句,句子主语是 A rapid intercity transport network,谓语是 has been put in place,featuring 作为现在分词引导定语,起修饰限定的作用,进一步强调是以高速铁路、城际铁路和高等级公路为主体的城际快速交通网络。

(3) Highlighting the need for integrated transport terminals, a group of such projects have been completed, such as the Beijing Daxing and Shanghai Hongqiao hubs, integrating airport transport seamlessly with high-speed and standard rail, and urban passenger transport.

翻译:通过强化一体化综合客运枢纽站建设,北京大兴、上海虹桥等一批综合交通枢纽建成,实现了高铁、轨道交通、城市客运、航空运输的无缝对接。

分析:该句为被动句,句子主语是 projects,谓语是 have been completed,Highlighting 作为现在分词放在句首起到状语的作用,阐明了构建 projects 的方式;此外,integrating 作为现在分词引导名词短语放在句末,进一步强调建设 projects 取得的成果。

# Exercises

## I. Reading and Understanding

**Decide whether the statements are true or false.**

(1) By the end of 2019, China had achieved more than 41 million km in the length of postal and express delivery services.

(2) The most prosperous cities are concentrated along the high-speed transport corridors.

(3) The logistics corridors are only used to transport energy such as gas and coal.

(4) Logistics parks and freight terminals are modified to achieve multilevel transport.

(5) China has made efforts to carry out a comprehensive and multidimensional transportation network to accelerate its social and economic development.

(6) The urban road network is only made of express ways and arterial roads, since they are friendly to green travel.

## II. Dealing with Unfamiliar Words

**Fill in the blanks in the following sentences with the correct form of the words and phrases from the box.**

| accelerate   accessibility   configure   total   approximate   thriving   populous |
| trunk   logistics   give...full play   foster   allocate |

(1) These documents are not _____ to the public.

(2) In 2005, college enrollments _____ some 5,400.

(3) His story _____ to the facts that we already know.

(4) Beijing is one of China's most _____ cities.

(5) Exposure to the sun can _____ the ageing process.

(6) They have _____ over 60 children during the past ten years.

(7) That's a good concept, and I think we should _____ it _____ in our new ad campaign.

(8) He _____ on hard work.

(9) We need to _____ the new system and reassign users and data.

(10) A _____ firm was hired for the deliveries.

(11) Over a 1,000 miles of new _____ roads and motorways have been built.

(12) More resources are being _____ to the project.

## III. Translating the Paragraph into English

中国五年前根本没有高速铁路。但是现在高铁列车的票经常很快就售罄，尽管发车间隔比较短。人们能够很方便地以两倍于美国火车最高速的速度在全国周游。高速铁路系统的运营非常成功，它运载的乘客数量是全国民航系统的两倍。中国有世界上最先进的、低排放的快速运输系统之一,而做到这一点仅仅用了五年。

## Ⅳ. Developing Critical Thinking

**Work in pairs and discuss the questions.**

(1) What transport means are there in your city?

(2) What do you think of the transport conditions in China?

(3) Can you suggest any other ways to improve the transport system in China?

扫码看答案

# Text B　CRH380A High Speed Train

CRH380A is high speed rolling stock which was developed by the China South Locomotive & Rolling Stock Corporation (CSR). It is one among the four train models designed to be operated at a speed of 380 km/h on the newly built Chinese high speed lines.

It is being manufactured by CSR Qingdao Sifang Locomotive & Rolling Stock. The train was put into regular operation on the Shanghai-Nanjing high speed railway line and Shanghai-Hangzhou high speed railway line from October 2010. It was put into daily service along the Wuhan-Guangzhou high-speed railway in December 2010.

It is the world record holder in the fastest train category, hitting a speed of 486.1 km/h on the world's longest high speed line in China.

## China's High Speed Railway Proposal and Development

The proposal to design a high speed train set started in early 2001. In February 2008, the Chinese Ministry of Science and Ministry of Railway signed an agreement on development of innovative high speed trains.

It was planned that a new generation high speed train would be developed which could continuously operate at a speed of 350 km/h. The project was included in the 11th Five Year Plan. The train sets were built and put into tests by early 2010.

## Design of the Chinese CRH380A Train

The design work was carried out in four main categories: schematic drawing, technological planning, structuring and building, and experimentation. Based on the analysis, an optimized sub-system design was put forward. More than 20 designs were shortlisted and were sent for further optimization and simulation. Around 1,000 technical tests in 17 specific areas, such as dynamic performance, pantograph, aerodynamic and traction performance, were conducted.

The technology to increase the maximum speed of the train was discovered through research carried out at various universities of China and was fed into the CSR's design.

The body is integrally welded with aluminium alloy and is shaped with a fish head-like structure in the front. The rotating paraboloid wedge structure cuts down aerodynamic resistance and mean energy consumption throughout the runtime. It also increases the amount of regenerated energy.

The new generation high speed electric multiple unit uses the electro pneumatic compound brake mode in which the train will use most of the regenerative braking energy. In the mean time, the traction motor will convert the energy into required power by means of a power generator. As a result of this, the maximum power of the train increases by 50%, which helps in terms of exceptional energy saving.

The train is designed to be completely vibration free. The train bogies are designed to be safe and reliable. They can withstand and run through a critical speed of 550 km/h. They are also incorporated with an advanced noise control technology by using new sound absorbing and insulating materials in the construction.

## Features of the New Generation High-speed Rolling Stock

The new generation train set comprises of various lounges and deluxe six seat compartments. It has a separate dining car called the Bistro Bar where snacks and selected meals are served. There are also separate bar counters where passengers can have a drink if they wish to.

"It is being manufactured by CSR Qingdao Sifang Locomotive & Rolling Stock."

A VIP sightseeing zone is adjacent to the driver's cab. It has an electronic curtain for which the water fog layer on the glass of the electronic curtain disappears instantly on the pressing of a button and gives a view of the running train from the driver's angle.

Each seat in the train is equipped with a display, dashboard, reading lamp and power port. Rotating seats are installed throughout the compartment.

Special facilities are provided for disabled people. One disabled toilet per compartment is installed with facilities such as an automatic door with on-off button, barrier free wheel car passage, handrail for the disabled and infant care table.

## Orders and Deliveries of CSR's Trains

CSR was awarded a contract worth $215.77 million by Hong Kong-based MTR to supply the CRH380A train sets to operate on the Guangzhou-Shenzhen-Hong Kong express rail link which is expected to be functional by 2015. The train sets will be customized according to MTR requirements.

CSR has delivered 40 train sets for operations on Shanghai-Hangzhou, Shanghai-Nanjing and Wuhan-Guangzhou high-speed railways in January 2011. About 67 EMUs are running along the Beijing-Shanghai high-speed railway, of which 21 were delivered in August 2011.

**Source**:

https://www.railway-technology.com/projects/crh380a-high-speed-china/.

## Language Studies

### I. Useful Expressions

(1) aerodynamic     *adj.* 空气动力学的

(2) brake     *n.* 刹车

(3) customize     *v.* 定做,按客户具体要求制造

(4) experimentation     *n.* 试验

(5) incorporate     *v.* 合并;混合

(6) insulating     *adj.* 绝缘的;隔热的

(7) manufacture     *v.* 制造,加工

(8) optimize     *v.* 使优化;充分利用

(9) put into operation     使生效;使运转

(10) rolling stock     (铁路上运行的)全部车辆(包括机车、车厢等)

(11) schematic drawing     示意图

(12) shortlist     *v.* 把……列入入围名单

(13) traction     *n.* (车辆)牵引力

(14) weld     *v.* 焊接;使成整体

## Ⅱ. Difficult Sentences

(1) The technology to increase the maximum speed of the train was discovered through research carried out at various universities of China and was fed into the CSR's design.

**翻译**:提升列车最高时速的技术由中国各大高校进行研发并应用到 CSR 设计中。

**分析**:该句是由 and 连接的并列句。句子的主语是 The technology,谓语动词是 was discovered 和 was fed into, through 作介词,用来引出技术被发现的方式。carried out 是过去分词作定语,起到修饰限定 research 的作用,说明研究是由中国多所高校开展。

(2) It has an electronic curtain for which the water fog layer on the glass of the electronic curtain disappears instantly on the pressing of a button and gives a view of the running train from the driver's angle.

**翻译**:VIP 观光区设有电子幕帘,旅客按动按钮后,电子幕帘玻璃的一层水雾立即消失,旅客可以以司机的视角观看列车运行。

**分析**:该句是由 and 连接的并列句。句子的主语是 It,指代 a VIP sightseeing zone,谓语动词是 has 和 gives,宾语分别为 an electronic curtain 和 a view of the running train,其中 for which 引导限定性定语从句,形容是什么样的电子幕帘。在这个定语从句中,主语是 the water fog layer on the glass of the electronic curtain,谓语动词是 disappears,介词 on 引导时间状语,阐明一按动按钮,水雾就会即刻消失。

# Exercises

## Ⅰ. Reading and Understanding

**Choose the best answer to each question.**

(1) What is the highest speed of CRH380A train set?

A. 380 km/h

B. 350 km/h

C. 486.1 km/h

D. 550 km/h

(2) According to the passage, which of the following is NOT TRUE about the CRH380A train set?

A. It is the most safety train category.

B. It was designed to run at a speed of 380 km/h on Chinese high speed lines.

C. It was developed and manufactured by CSR.

D. Its design work mainly includes schematic drawing, technological planning, structuring and building, and experimentation.

(3) Why was CRH380 designed with a rotating paraboloid wedge structure?

A. To look like a fish head

B. To reduce aerodynamic resistance

C. To decrease the amount of regenerated energy

D. To keep vibration free

(4) Which of the following facilities could NOT be found on the high-speed train set?

A. Disabled toilet

B. Reading lamp

C. Rotating seats

D. Baby care room

(5) What do we learn from the passage?

A. CRH380 train sets operate only on Shanghai-Hangzhou, Shanghai-Nanjing and Wuhan-Guangzhou high-speed railways.

B. Passengers could buy snacks and meals at separate bar counters.

C. The proposal to design a high speed train set started in 2008.

D. CRH 380 train sets have advantages of high speed, safety, and comfort.

## II. Dealing with Unfamiliar Words

**Fill in the blanks in the following sentences with the correct form of the words and phrases from the box.**

| put...into operation   innovative   optimize   shortlist   regenerate |
| adjacent...to   simulate   incorporate   insulate   exceptional |

(1) We finally _____ the machine _____ after spending all morning repairing it.

(2) The scientists make efforts to _____ computers for speed and memory.

(3) We have _____ all the latest safety features into the design.

(4) There is a row of houses immediately _____ the factory.

(5) There will be a prize for the most _____ design.

(6) The money will be used to _____ the commercial heart of the town.

(7) The film is on the _____ for Best Picture.

(8) Until now the industry has been _____ from economic realities.

(9) An important part of training is role-play and the _____ of court cases.

(10) At the age of five, he showed _____ talent as a musician.

## III. Translating the Paragraph into English

中国目前拥有世界上最大、最快的高速铁路网。高铁列车的运行速度还将继续提高,更多的城市将修建高铁站。高铁大大缩短了人们出行的时间。相对飞机而言,高铁列车的突出优势在于准时,因为基本不受天气或者交通管制的影响。高铁极大地改变了中国人的生活方式。如今,它已经成为很多人商务旅行的首选交通工具。越来越多的人也在假日乘高铁外出旅游。还有不少年轻人选择在一个城市工作,而在邻近城市居住,每天乘高铁上下班。

## IV. Developing Critical Thinking

**Work in pairs and discuss the questions.**

(1) What kind(s) of transport do you usually use?

(2) Why do many people in China travel by high-speed trains?

（3）What do you think about the advantages and disadvantages of high-speed trains?

扫码看答案

# Unit 3
# China's New Architecture

## Text A  Wuhan's Huoshenshan Hospital: A Symbol of Chinese Spirit

"Chinese constructors would like to share all its experience in designing Wuhan's hospitals to countries in need," said a technical expert that worked on the Huoshenshan Hospital, the emergency field hospital for treating COVID-19 patients that had been constructed within only 10 days in Wuhan, Central China's Hubei Province.

Xiao Wei, deputy director of the CITIC General Institute of Architectural Design and Research and coordinator of the technical support team for the construction of the field hospital, told the *Global Times* that they have received requests about building similar hospitals from some countries, and might cooperate with these nations on some epidemic prevention projects.

"We are pleased to participate in these projects abroad and share our wisdom and designs with the world," he said.

According to Xiao, the original blueprints and drawings of Huoshenshan Hospital have been made available to the public, keeping some dishonest companies from using fake blueprints to cheat clients. He also said that the authentic blueprints proved that the claim made by some media outlets that Huoshenshan Hospital was designed by a Japanese designer was false.

However, although the resources and experience from China have been made available to the world, the standards for building hospitals vary from country to country and the successful cases of building a hospital within 10 days cannot necessarily be replicated 100 percent.

"The standards of building a hospital for curing infectious diseases when it comes to its structure, energy conservation, building materials and many other aspects are different between different countries. Although we have made the blueprints available, other countries still need to take time to make some adjustments that are in line with the conditions in their own countries," Xiao said.

The CITIC General Institute of Architectural Design and Research also helped design several modular hospitals as well as complete a specific design standard for the adaptation of this type of hospital. Modular hospitals also played an important role in containing the COVID-19 outbreak. Importantly, they achieved the goal of what designers called the "five zeros"—zero in-patient deaths, zero medical staff infections, zero recurrences after treatment, zero safety accidents and zero occupant complaints.

## Adjusting to Local Conditions

The Huoshenshan Hospital was based on the design of the Xiaotangshan Hospital in Beijing, which was built to treat SARS patients back in 2003, with some adjustments and improvements made to the design to accommodate the local climate in Wuhan, construction speed, 5G technology, the ventilation system and isolation measures to protect medical staff and patients.

For example, considering that the hospital was going to be built near a lake, the team added an anti-seepage membrane to isolate the entire hospital from its environment, ensuring that any medical waste would not contaminate the lake or soil.

The hospital also included 5G coverage and wired broadband, which were used to connect to a remote consultation platform that had been set up so that experienced doctors in other provinces around China would be able to conduct remote consultations with patients in Wuhan. He added that the live streaming of the construction of the hospital and the millions of Chinese viewers played an important role in giving staff the encouragement they needed to complete the difficult task.

"It is unbelievable to see that millions of people are supervising your work online.

Some suggestions from Chinese netizens were good, but due to time constraints, we couldn't implement all their suggestions."

Xiao is scheduled to introduce the design of the Huoshenshan Hospital later this year to the China Pavilion at the Venice Biennale 2020 themed on *Courtyards: From Big to Small, How We Live Together*. A juxtaposition of Huoshenshan Hospital and the legendary Imperial Palace will show the connections between the two that are rooted in Chinese architectural philosophy.

## Solidarity amid Difficulty

According to Xiao, the biggest challenge they faced when building Huoshenshan Hospital was time. Usually, it takes almost a year to design a hospital due to the sheer amount of research needed.

However, the great urgency this time did not allow them to follow their normal routine. They only spent 60 hours drawing up the blueprints for the Huoshenshan Hospital and constantly making adjustments as they learned more about the site.

The design team was divided into two parts. One is dedicated to design and the other to cooperating with workers at the construction site. The members of both teams were top designers and engineers in various fields including water supply and heating. Their experience and knowledge allowed them to cooperate and quickly make decisions on what problems could be solved right on the spot. They also shared their evolving experience with the team in charge of building the Leishenshan Hospital, the sister field hospital constructed after Huoshenshan.

Xiao said he was impressed by how companies shouldered their responsibilities during this crisis. They contributed all of their best resources such as medical equipment, televisions and air conditioners and delivered them to the hospital on time, which helped with the construction immensely.

"Building the Huoshenshan Hospital in just 10 days is a unique accomplishment in the world. It shows China's highly improved construction ability and that Chinese enterprises have very strong capabilities in logistics, which other countries may not be able to replicate," he said.

## Chinese Spirit

Xiao said that the project allowed him to feel the spirit of the Chinese people. He said he feels that the hospital should be converted into an exhibition center or a museum so others may feel this spirit as well.

"It might be a good idea to change the Huoshenshan Hospital into a museum to show the stories that happened there and convey the spirit of the Chinese people as they can unite to fight against the rampaging novel coronavirus."

He noted that he was touched by the hard-working female designers who went to the site, unafraid of the possibility of getting infected. He noted that about 40 to 50 percent of the designers who participated in the design of emergency hospitals such as Huoshenshan Hospital and other modular hospitals were females.

He was also moved by the workers who spent days and nights building the hospital during the Chinese New Year holiday and the sense of responsibility of those large state-owned enterprises which participated voluntarily without consideration of reward.

"The workers are great people. I think it is very important that an ordinary person can stand up and offer help at a special time like this. This is our Chinese spirit, and we used that spirit to make a global miracle."

**Source:**

https://www.globaltimes.cn/content/1183849.shtml.

# Language Focus

## Ⅰ. Useful Expressions

(1) accommodate  　　　　　　　　*n.* 容纳;为……提供空间
(2) anti-seepage membrane 　　　　防渗膜
(3) blueprint 　　　　　　　　　　*n.* (建筑、机器等的)蓝图
(4) contaminate 　　　　　　　　　*v.* 污染;弄脏
(5) COVID-19/coronavirus 　　　　 *n.* 冠状病毒

(6) epidemic　　　　　　　　　　　　　　 *n.* 流行病

(7) field hospital　　　　　　　　　　　　 临时伤病医院；野战医院

(8) in line with　　　　　　　　　　　　　（与……）一致；（与……）相符

(9) juxtaposition　　　　　　　　　　　　 *n.* 并置，并列

(10) live streaming　　　　　　　　　　　 *n.* 视频直播；现场直播

(11) logistics　　　　　　　　　　　　　　*n.* 后勤；物流；组织工作

(12) media outlet　　　　　　　　　　　　 媒体；媒介

(13) modular hospital　　　　　　　　　　 方舱医院

(14) netizen　　　　　　　　　　　　　　 *n.* 网民

(15) on the spot　　　　　　　　　　　　　当场；在现场；马上

(16) outbreak　　　　　　　　　　　　　　*n.* （暴力、疾病等坏事的）爆发

(17) recurrence　　　　　　　　　　　　　*n.* 重现；复发

(18) remote consultation platform　　　　　远程会诊平台

(19) SARS　　　　　　　　　　　　　　　 *abbr.* 严重急性呼吸综合征；"非典"

(20) ventilation　　　　　　　　　　　　　*n.* 通风设备；空气流通

## Ⅱ. Difficult Sentences

(1) ...the original blueprints and drawings of Huoshenshan Hospital have been made available to the public, keeping some dishonest companies from using fake blueprints to cheat clients.

**翻译**：……火神山医院的原始设计图和图纸已经向公众公开，以防止一些不良公司使用伪造的设计图来欺骗客户。

**分析**：该句中，主语+have been+made+available to 是由 make 构成的现在完成时被动语态，可译为"向某人提供某物"。keeping 引导的内容作伴随状语来修饰主句，表示动作发生的原因，即公开火神山医院设计图纸的原因。

(2) The Huoshenshan Hospital was based on the design of the Xiaotangshan Hospital in Beijing, which was built to treat SARS patients back in 2003, with some adjustments and improvements made to the design to accommodate the local climate in Wuhan, construction speed, 5G technology, the ventilation system and isolation measures to protect medical staff and patients.

**翻译**：北京小汤山医院于2003年建成，用于治疗SARS患者，火神山医院以此

为基础,并进行了一些调整和改进,以适应武汉当地的气候、建设速度、5G 技术、通风系统和隔离措施,以保护医护人员和患者。

**分析:**该句的主干结构为主语+was based on,可译为"以……为根据""根据……""基于……"。which 引导非限定性定语从句,对 the design of the Xiaotangshan Hospital in Beijing 进行补充说明。with+名词+to do 构成复合结构,作伴随状语,进一步修饰主语。

(3) It might be a good idea to change the Huoshenshan Hospital into a museum to show the stories that happened there and convey the spirit of the Chinese people as they can unite to fight against the rampaging novel coronavirus.

**翻译:**将火神山医院改建为博物馆不失为一个好办法,用以展示在那里曾发生过的故事,并且传达中国人民的精神,因为他们能够团结一致对抗猖獗的新型冠状病毒。

**分析:**该句的结构为 It is +n. +to do,其中 It 为形式主语,真正的主语是后面的不定式形式。to show... and convey... 为不定式结构作状语,表行目的和结果。as 在此句中引导原因状语从句,进一步解释前句提到的"中国人民的精神"。

# Exercises

## I. Reading and Understanding

**Decide whether the statements are true or false.**

(1) The original blueprints of Huoshenshan Hospital have been made public because Chinese constructors would like to share all experience to countries in need.

(2) Other countries can copy the design of Huoshenshan Hospital directly without changing any details at all.

(3) When building Huoshenshan Hospital, the biggest challenge was the lack of time.

(4) The Huoshenshan Hospital was changed into a museum to show the stories that happened there and convey the spirit of the Chinese people.

(5) Many female designers participated in the design of Huoshenshan Hospital, unafraid of getting infected.

## Ⅱ. Dealing with Unfamiliar Words

**Complete the following sentences with expressions given in the box below. Change the form where necessary.**

| on the spot   dedicated to   draw up   due to   root in   in line with |
| cooperate with   scheduled to   converted into   set up |

(1) Following Monday's deadline to submit nominations, the Nobel committee will _____ a shortlist of candidates before a winner is chosen in October.

(2) Their mission is _____ promoting awareness and preservation of coastal margins and the marine environment through the disciplines of the sciences and the arts.

(3) A new mini-laboratory system can identify the virus within roughly 40 minutes and makes it possible to conduct up to 60 tests a day right _____ where samples are taken.

(4) Schools which are _____ resume in-person classes for Grade 9 and above from Monday will be full-day regular classes between 10 am and 4:30 pm.

(5) _____ the COVID-19 pandemic, this meeting will be conducted virtually.

(6) Across India, weddings are a significant milestone, deeply _____ traditions and culture even today.

(7) Deputy director called on the owners of public and private facilities to _____ the authority to serve the public interest.

(8) A former public building which has planning permission to be _____ 12 flats has been put on the market.

(9) The member nations will _____ a working group to discuss whether to admit Britain.

(10) _____ the State Government's resolve to have zero tolerance against corruption, the CM today approved the proposal of suspension of Deputy Registrar, Deoghar, Rahul Chaubey on Saturday.

## Ⅲ. Translating the Paragraph into English

火神山医院的结构和布局是高度模块化的。病房楼采用箱体结构进行装配化组合,形成医疗单元。医护人员和患者的空间被整齐划分,最大限度地降低交叉感染的风险。所有的病房都是用防火和抗燃材料建造的集装箱结构,经过精心设计,在工厂预制,在现场组装,就像组装一套积木。

## Ⅳ. Developing Critical Thinking

**Work in pairs and discuss the question.**

From the monumental structures to the residences and buildings that make up the fabric of a city, architecture has stood as a representation of society. In what ways do you think architecture can reflect a culture? Give an example.

扫码看答案

# Text B  Hong Kong-Zhuhai-Macao Bridge: A Megaproject Full of Chinese Wisdom

After eight years of difficult construction, China's much-anticipated Hong Kong-Zhuhai-Macao Bridge (HZMB) is slated for traffic operation on the upcoming Wednesday. The 55-kilometer bridge, crowned one of the "seven wonders of the modern world" and "Mt. Qomolangma" in the field of bridge construction, is one of the world's most challenging megaprojects.

"The construction scale and difficulty of the HZMB is the biggest, compared to other existing cross-sea bridge-tunnel transportation cluster projects," said Su Quanke, chief engineer of the HZMB Authority.

With the devotion of over 200 R&D institutions and thousands of sci-tech personnel, the project has been granted over 1,000 patents, pushing the boundaries of possibility over and over again.

## Bridge, Island and Tunnel, All Integral

The world's longest sea-based project comprises four parts, including a 22.9-kilometer steel bridge, two artificial islands, a submerged sea tunnel extending for 6.7 kilometers at a depth of 40 meters, as well as leading bridges that connect the bridge to the cities.

For a bridge project, designers prefer to build all the structure on the ground, and only opt to the tunnel when there is no alternative.

However, for the HZMB, the most feasible design is to integrate bridge, island and tunnel to form a complete cross-sea channel.

"The Pearl River Estuary holds a world-level shipping channel where around 5,000 vessels get through at its busiest time of the day. Smooth traffic should be guaranteed. And the location is near the Hong Kong International Airport. With about 2,000 flights taking off and landing at the airport, the bridge cannot be built too high for safety reasons," said Meng Fanchao, chief designer of the HZMB project. "But you cannot have a submerged sea tunnel without any support. That forced us to build the artificial islands."

Chinese engineers blazed a trail in installing deep-immersed tunnel tubes. "There is no model for us to refer to as all the cases are shallow-buried tubes," said Su.

"Due to lack of experience, the installation of the first tube lasted for 96 hours, and we did not take a rest for four days and five nights," said Yin Haiqing, deputy manager of the Project Management Department for Island and Tunnel. "Everyone was exhausted when we made it."

The 6.7-kilometer tunnel is the world's longest submerged sea tunnel.

Two artificial islands, covering an area of 200,000 square meters, help create a smooth transition between bridge sections and tunnels.

Different from traditional island reclaimed from the sea, the engineers "put 120 steel cylinders with a 22-meter diameter into the seabed, make out the shape of an island, and fill the island with soil," Su said, introducing the innovative way they adopted to build the artificial island, saying it was firmer, more efficient and friendly to the marine ecology.

The giant structure is also 55 meters high, as tall as an 18-story building. It weighs 550 tons, roughly the weight of an Airbus A-380 plane.

## Building Blocks

The HZMB is formed of box girders, amounting to 420,000 tons of steel—roughly the weight of 60 Eiffel Towers or 10 Beijing National Stadiums (the Bird's Nest).

Many of the steel components, such as the piers, pylons and immersed tubes, were made by China's large self-developed equipment, and then shipped to the construction site. Assembling the precast components is just like building blocks, but with much more difficulty.

The constructors even spun a steel pylon with a height of 160 meters and a weight of over 3,000 tons at 90 degrees above the sea, an unprecedented practice in the history of the world's bridge construction.

"Such an integrated design would not have been possible if the country's overall research capability and equipment level had not advanced to the current level," said Su.

The bridge also made a first in China touse robot welding. "The multi-head welding avoids uneven thermal distribution, eliminating internal stress caused by the welding process," said Chai Rui, deputy chief engineer of the HZMB Authority.

## Longer Lifespan, Safer Design

The designers made another breakthrough in the lifespan of the bridge. Bridges in China are usually designed to serve for no longer than 100 years, and the sea environment will largely shorten the lifespan of architectures due to high humidity and salinity.

To address the problem, the designers used new materials and new technologies like concrete reinforcement and rust resistance.

They also applied fire prevention and accident rescue facilities for the bridge. The designers built an experiment platform for the submerged sea tunnel to conduct combustion tests of vehicles. Three years of experiments show that the fireproof facility can ensure that the immersed tubes won't be destroyed for two hours under 1,200 degrees Celsius.

The artificial island also has a marine rescue platform, which will send a rescue team within three minutes to the tunnel and five to seven minutes to the bridge if an accident happens.

"The megaproject is also the best place for the application of China's latest technologies," said Su. "We hope more large projects can play their roles in leading the transformation and upgrading of China's manufacturing."

**Source:**
https://news.cgtn.com/news/3d3d774d354d444d30457a6333566d54/share_p.html.

# Language Focus

## I. Useful Expressions

(1) Beijing National Stadium     鸟巢;国家体育馆

(2) blaze a trail                    开辟道路；领先
(3) box girder                       ［建］箱形梁
(4) combustion                       *n.* 燃烧
(5) concrete reinforcement           *n.* 混凝土钢筋
(6) Eiffel Tower                     埃菲尔铁塔
(7) feasible                         *adj.* 可行的；行得通的
(8) humidity                         *n.* 湿度
(9) integrate                        *v.* （使）合并，成为一体
(10) lifespan                        *n.* 寿命；预期使用期限
(11) marine ecology                  ［生态］海洋生态学
(12) megaproject                     *n.* 大型项目，大型工程
(13) Pearl River Estuary             珠江河口
(14) personnel                       *n.* 人员
(15) pier                            *n.* 柱子；桥墩
(16) precast                         *adj.* （尤指建筑用水泥）预制的
(17) pylon                           *n.* （架高压输电线的）电缆塔
(18) R&D                             *abbr.* 研究与开发（research and development）
(19) reclaim                         *v.* 开垦；改造
(20) rust resistance                 *n.* 耐锈蚀性
(21) salinity                        *n.* 盐度
(22) sci-tech                        *n.* 科技
(23) slate for                       预定；计划；安排
(24) transition                      *n.* 过渡；转变
(25) unprecedented                   *adj.* 空前的；史无前例的

## Ⅱ. Difficult Sentences

(1) The 55-kilometer bridge, crowned one of the "seven wonders of the modern world" and "Mt. Qomolangma" in the field of bridge construction, is one of the world's most challenging megaprojects.

**翻译**：这座55千米长的大桥是世界上最具挑战的大型工程之一，被誉为"现代世界七大奇迹"之一和桥梁建设领域的"珠穆朗玛峰"。

**分析**：该句骨干结构为 The 55-kilometer bridge is one of the world's most challenging megaprojects,crowned 在这里是过去分词短语作非限制性定语,相当于非限制性定语从句省略 which is,可译为"被誉为,获得……称号"。

(2) With the devotion of over 200 R&D institutions and thousands of sci-tech personnel, the project has been granted over 1,000 patents, pushing the boundaries of possibility over and over again.

**翻译**:在 200 多家研发机构和数千名科技人员的投入下,该工程已获专利 1,000 余项,不断突破可能性的极限。

**分析**:该句的主干结构是 the project has been granted over 1,000 patents,主句前的 With+名词短语作伴随状语,表示工程所获专利是在这种状态下发生的。主句后 pushing 引导的现在分词短语也是伴随状语,它表示动作"突破极限"是伴随着主句的动作而发生的。

# Exercises

## Ⅰ. Reading and Understanding

**Choose the best answer to each question.**

(1) Which of the following is not part of the sea-based project?

A. A 22.9-kilometer steel bridge.

B. 6.7-kilometer sea tunnel.

C. 120 steel cylinders with a 22-meter diameter into the seabed.

D. Two artificial islands.

(2) What is the advantage of robot welding?

A. It avoids uneven thermal distribution.

B. It eliminates external stress caused by the welding process.

C. It extends the lifespan of the bridge.

D. It is firmer, more efficient and friendly to the marine ecology.

(3) The designers tried to increase the lifespan of the bridge. Which of the

following is not true?

A. They used new materials and new technologies.

B. They spun a steel pylon above the sea.

C. They applied fire prevention and accident rescue facilities for the bridge.

D. They constructed a marine rescue platform.

## II. Dealing with Unfamiliar Words

### Choose the word that best fits in the blank.

(1) Students are living in _____ times where there is a high level of stress, fear and anxiety.

A. incredible    B. unpredictable    C. unprecedented    D. unfeasible

(2) The star AU Microscopii is no more than 22 million years old, in other words, only a few months if the _____ of a star was reduced to that of a human being.

A. lifespan    B. length    C. lifelong    D. lifestyle

(3) The U.S. does not allow its former citizens to _____ U.S. nationality once it has been renounced.

A. recycle    B. reaffirm    C. request    D. reclaim

(4) European allies urge smooth _____ to new unified Libyan authority.

A. transfer    B. transition    C. transportation    D. transaction

(5) Because exercise is good for us at any time of day—but only if we _____ keep doing it.

A. insist on    B. opt to    C. opt for    D. insist to

(6) The central bank has been assessing whether the policy could work in the U.K. and concluded that it was "operationally _____".

A. feasible    B. probable    C. eligible    D. sustainable

(7) The WHO team has talked with relevant administrative _____, experts,

business owners, residents and media representatives there.

A. gang  B. crew  C. staff  D. personnel

(8) Sarah Thomas will _____ for female officials everywhere on Sunday when she becomes the first woman to officiate at the Super Bowl.

A. show up  B. make her debut  C. blaze a trail  D. in the spotlight

## III. Translating the Paragraph into Chinese

The Hong Kong-Zhuhai-Macao Bridge (HZMB), being situated at the waters of Lingdingyang of Pearl River Estuary, is a mega-size sea crossing linking the Hong Kong Special Administrative Region (HKSAR), Zhuhai City of Guangdong Province and Macao Special Administrative Region. The functions of the bridge are to meet the demand of passenger and freight land transport among Hong Kong, the mainland (particularly the region of Pearl River West) and Macao, to establish a new land transport link between the east and west banks of the Pearl River, and to enhance the economic and sustainable development of the three places.

## IV. Developing Critical Thinking

**Work in pairs and discuss the questions.**

(1) What were the challenges during the construction of Hong Kong-Zhuhai-Macao Bridge (HZMB)?

(2) How will the Hong Kong-Macao-Zhuhai Bridge stimulate the development of Hong Kong, Macau, Zhuhai and the whole Greater Bay Area?

扫码看答案

# Unit 4
# China's New Commerce

## Text A  What It's Like to Live in a Cashless Society

Over a decade ago, Alipay launched in China, promising easy online transactions for all. A few years later, Chinese super app WeChat introduced a similar mobile payment service called WeChat Pay to its millions of users. Today, the two platforms are ubiquitous on smartphones all over the country, driving a mobile-driven revolution that has made China one of the most cashless societies in the world. Those living there say they've survived for years without a wallet.

China is home to about 1.4 billion people, and hundreds of millions of them rely on smartphones to pay for anything and everything. Most businesses have a QR code, which customers can scan with payment apps to make a purchase. This has become so widespread that the government has had to crack down on merchants who refuse cash payments from customers, stressing that the Chinese yuan is still the statutory currency and legal tender of China.

Shanghai-based Toby Graham, 40, works for an international accounting firm and to him, it's impossible to imagine going back to cash. "I couldn't give you a date for when I last used cash here in China, but it's definitely been years," Graham told VICE World News. He has been living in China for eight years and has watched the nationwide takeover of WeChat and Alipay. By 2017, he had stopped using ATMs.

"In the last four months, because of work, I have traveled to seven major cities in China and all I took with me was a passport, some clothes, and my phone," Graham shared. "At no point did I need to take cash out. I don't even have a wallet."

Graham explained that while he also has his credit card on him, he only uses it in the event that he loses his phone.

"The phone is how you do everything. I use it to pay for utility and bills, to pay rent to my landlord, to shop online, and to buy groceries at the supermarket. I can't think of one thing you can't do with your phone here," he said.

The use of mobile payment apps has even penetrated remote villages. According to Chinese market research firm Daxue Consulting, nearly half of the country's rural population reportedly uses mobile payment services regularly. In 2017, transactions through non-banking mobile payment services in rural areas totaled 42.9 trillion Chinese yuan ($6.64 trillion).

"I've seen really small businesses—I'm talking about those small fruit shops you see on the side of the road, or the guy who makes fried noodles and pushes a trolley down the street—and they don't even accept cash anymore," Graham said. "I see beggars all the time and they'll carry QR codes with them which you can scan to give them money."

While many are optimistic about the idea of a cashless society, there are others who worry that it leaves some communities behind. San Francisco-based consumer finance expert Erica Sandberg has the same concern.

"The move toward an entirely cashless society absolutely leaves the un-banked behind. Not everybody has a credit or debit card, or a smartphone equipped with a mobile wallet," Sandberg told VICE World News.

"A physical wallet that you load up with bills and then pay for things as you go along is a powerful process. It's tangible," she added. "You can watch your money disappear as you spend, so you are more likely to be careful."

Sandberg also warned that going entirely cashless could impinge on personal freedom and privacy. "Being able to make a purchase that is not tracked is important. Cash offers the ability to conduct transactions that marketers and other companies can't monitor," she said.

But privacy concerns don't always lead to users limiting their use of technology, especially during the pandemic, when contactless transactions are preferred. Richard Hartung, managing director of Singapore-based financial consultancy firm Transcart, said that non-cash transactions in Asia have been rising despite privacy issues because most people prioritize convenience.

"Digital payments have grown due to the growing number of options available, the lower costs of digital payments, and more recently, because of the pandemic, which has accelerated digitization," Hartung told VICE World News.

He also said that while China is way ahead of the movement in Asia, it's only a matter of time before other countries go cashless.

"Other parts of Asia will catch up. Convenient apps help. Government support helps. Innovation helps. But digitization amidst COVID-19 has been the biggest push."

**Source:**

https://www.vice.com/en_us/article/93wz3p/cashless-country-experience-china-sweden-korea-wechat-alipay-swish-samsungpay.

# Language Focus

## I. Useful Expressions

(1) consultancy           n. 咨询
(2) contactless           adj. 非接触式的
(3) currency              n. 货币
(4) innovation            n. 创新；改革
(5) pandemic              n. 全球性流行病
(6) platform              n. 平台
(7) prioritize            v. 优先
(8) QR code               n. 二维码
(9) smartphone            n. 智能手机
(10) widespread           adj. 广泛的；普遍的

## II. Difficult Sentences

(1) Today, the two platforms are ubiquitous on smartphones all over the country,

driving a mobile-driven revolution that has made China one of the most cashless societies in the world.

**翻译**：如今，这两个应用在全中国的智能手机上随处可见，推动了一场移动驱动的技术革命，从而使中国成为世界上无现金化程度最高的国家之一。

**分析**：该句的主语是 the two platforms，driving 作为现在分词引导分句，起补充说明和修饰限定的作用，进一步强调 platform 所引发的是一场 revolution，即革命。revolution 之后为一个限制性定语从句，形容是什么样的革命。其引导词 that 在从句中作主语，通过使用 make sth. 这一短语结构，让 China 充当直接宾语，societies 充当宾语补足语来描述革命对中国产生的影响。该定语从句的其他部分则均为 societies 的修饰语。

（2）This has become so widespread that the government has had to crack down on merchants who refuse cash payments from customers, stressing that the Chinese yuan is still the statutory currency and legal tender of China.

**翻译**：这种情况已经非常普遍，以至于政府不得不打击拒收客户现金的商家，并强调纸质人民币仍然是中国的法定流通货币。

**分析**：该句主要结构为 so...that，意为"如此……以至于"，描述语义的递进关系。从 who 开始引导的是一个限制性定语从句，修饰限定 merchants，即形容什么样的商家。后面由 stressing 这一分词引导的分句对应的主语是 the government，该分句进一步展开说明中国政府保证现金流通的具体措施，即强调现金流通的法定性。that 后面所接的是强调的对象，即该句为一个宾语从句，宾语的全部内容均为政府所强调的内容。

（3）Digital payments have grown due to the growing number of options available, the lower costs of digital payments, and more recently, because of the pandemic, which has accelerated digitization.

**翻译**：由于可供选择的选项越来越多，数字支付的成本越来越低，以及最近的流行病加速了数字化，数字支付得到了发展。

**分析**：due to 意为"因为……"，跟在其后并列的几项均为原因，即解释数字支付发展的原因。and 通常连接最后一项，most recently 是时间状语，进一步限定最后一个原因 pandemic 是最近才发生的。which 引导的限制性定语从句则通过描述流行病是什么样的来明确其与电子化加速的因果关系，其中 which 在从句中作主语。

**Exercises**

## I. Reading and Understanding

**1. Choose the best answer to each question.**

(1) If Toby wants to use mobile payment services, what should he do?

A. Draw a QR code.

B. Scan the QR code with his mobile phone.

C. Ask others to help him scan the QR code.

D. Use Alipay and WeChat Pay at the same time.

(2) What does Toby think about mobile payment services?

A. It's not that convenient compared to credit card.

B. It's inconvenient to download all kinds of mobile payment apps.

C. It's not safety enough and he refuses to use it.

D. It makes it possible for him to travel without taking cash out.

(3) What do we learn from the passage?

A. The use of mobile payment apps has penetrated remote villages in China.

B. One can only use cash in small businesses.

C. All people are optimistic about the idea of a cashless society.

D. There is no point owning a wallet loading up with bills.

(4) Under what circumstances do people only use cash?

A. When they purchase in small businesses

B. When they go to travel

C. When they lose their mobile phones

D. When they live in rural area in China

(5) What can we learn from Hartung's words?

A. There will be a lot more other payment methods in the future.

B. COVID-19 pandemic has been accelerating the development of cashless.

C. Asian countries may not choose the same road as China in payment innovation.

D. Governments don't interfere with cash digitization.

**2. Decide whether the statements are true or false.**

(1) Alipay launched in China fifty years ago.

(2) Customers can scan QR codes with payment apps to make purchases.

(3) Merchants are not allowed to refuse cash payments from customers.

(4) Mobile payment services are not commonly used in remote villages in China.

(5) People are more likely to be careful using cash to purchase.

## Ⅱ. Translating the Paragraph into English

"无现金社会"虽然便利,但也存在很多弊端。首先,并非所有人都拥有智能手机;其次,使用电子支付可能会导致个人信息泄露;最后,电子支付可能会导致过度消费。虽然现金在当今社会的使用频率已经远不如电子货币,但我们仍然需要承认现金的"情感价值",并保持现金的正常流通。

## Ⅲ. Developing Critical Thinking

**Work in pairs and discuss the questions.**

(1) How do we balance the pros and cons of cashless society?

(2) Do you think saving money as cash or e-cash feels different? If so, what is the difference?

扫码看答案

# Text B  Xiabuxiabu

Xiabuxiabu is renovating outlets on the mainland to appeal to a young clientele.

Hotpot restaurant operator Xiabuxiabu is not going to let the pandemic get in its way. The company has formulated a strategy that will transform it into a fresh food delivery company in a "worst-case scenario", and it remains on track to open another 100 outlets this year, including a few overseas.

In case of any eventuality, especially during the Lunar New Year, the Beijing-based catering company has a contingency plan to turn over 1,000 outlets, most of which are situated close to residential areas, into a grocery delivery service. The company said it would use its waiters and chefs to sort, pack and deliver the fresh vegetables and meat ordered for its hotpot restaurants.

"We are not scared of the pandemic because we are prepared to face any unforeseen circumstances," said Zhao Yi, CEO of Hong Kong-listed Xiabuxiabu Catering Management China Holdings.

"In the event of a worst-case scenario, if everything shuts down again (because of lockdowns), all our restaurants can quickly turn into (a convenience store like) 7-Eleven or Dingdong Maicai, the fresh vegetable e-commerce platform, allowing us to serve consumers fresh meat and vegetables prepared for our hotpot."

Last year, when China implemented stringent lockdowns during the Lunar New Year to contain the pandemic, the restaurant sector was among the worst hit industries.

"What we learned in the past year is that you always need a plan B and to respond quickly as the world is changing fast," said Zhao.

The company is also pushing ahead with its expansion plan to launch 100 outlets this year, which will include its first overseas outlets in Thailand, Singapore and Malaysia. To appeal to free spending millennials, the company is introducing new decor for the restaurants, abandoning its dark orange interiors for the first time since its founding in 1998.

"In our new stores, everything, from wall to sofa, from table to cutlery, will be in white and light grey. The so-called Instagram-style is to cater to the millennials and 'Generation Z'—our new target consumers," she said.

As of June last year, Xiabuxiabu ranked as the largest hotpot chain on the mainland with 1,010 outlets, followed closely by Hong Kong-listed Haidilao with 935 outlets, according to their financial reports.

However, it faces increasing competition from hotpot chains like Xiaolongkan, Dalongyi and Diantaixiang, which have emerged from Sichuan province in the past few years.

In China, hotpot accounts for 17.5 percent of the 4 trillion yuan (US \$ 578 billion) dining sector, making it the largest segment in formal dining, according to a report by consulting firm iiMedia Research. There were some 516,000 hotpot restaurants in the country in 2019, estimates from China's on-demand service platform Meituan showed, with the figure likely to reach 900,000 by 2022.

"The hotpot restaurants can only make their mark if they can accurately position themselves in a specific niche market," said Dai Jiaxian, an analyst from Citic Securities.

Hotpot is a communal dining experience where large groups of friends and families cook plates of meat and vegetables in a soup at the centre of their table. But concerns that sharing food and gathering in confined spaces is helping to spread the coronavirus have affected the segment.

"We believe 'one person, one pot' to be the future," said Zhao, adding that this will help the company "target young spenders who like to pay for small portions and enjoy a healthy lifestyle".

Xiabuxiabu reported a loss of 252.1 million yuan for the first half of 2020 compared to a profit of 162.2 million yuan a year earlier, but it has seen an improvement as the year progressed, with revenues returning to 95 percent of pre-pandemic levels by October. Zhao said the company was likely to post a profit this year if the pandemic remains under control.

"The pandemic is a monster wreaking havoc on the industry. Only the nimblest will survive," Zhao said.

**Source:**

https://www.msn.com/en-xl/money/other/hotpot-chain-xiabuxiabu-plans-to-transform-into-a-fresh-food-delivery-platform-in-case-of-virus-surge-during-lunar-new-year/ar-BB1dsCay.

# Language Focus

## Ⅰ. Useful Expressions

(1) accurately            adv. 精确地
(2) communal              adj. 公共的
(3) emerge                v. 出现；显露
(4) formulate             v. 规划；构想
(5) interior              n. 内部
(6) millennial            n. 千禧一代
(7) outlet                n. 经销店；门店
(8) revenue               n. 收入；收益
(9) specific              adj. 特殊的；特定的
(10) stringent            adj. 严格的

## Ⅱ. Difficult Sentences

(1) The company has formulated a strategy that will transform it into a fresh food delivery company in a "worst-case scenario", and it remains on track to open another 100 outlets this year, including a few overseas.

**翻译：**该公司制定了一项战略，即在"最糟糕的情况"下将公司转化为新鲜食品外送公司。与此同时，公司还有望在今年新增100家门店，包括一些海外门店。

**分析：**strategy 为 formulate 的宾语，后文 that 引导的从句作为定语进一步说明是什么样的战略。在后文 and 引导的句子中，it 作代词指代前文的 the company，其后的内容均为公司的举措，且该句与前文的定语从句无关，与引导定语从句的主句形成并列关系。

(2) To appeal to free spending millennials, the company is introducing new decor for the restaurants, abandoning its dark orange interiors for the first time since its founding in 1998.

**翻译：**为吸引千禧一代的自主消费，该公司开始引入新的装饰，这也是其自

1998 年成立以来首次放弃橙色内饰。

**分析**:开头的不定式结构为目的状语,提示目的。后文用现在进行时态表示动作尚未完成,正在推进。abandoning 为现在分词,提示伴随性动作或状态,进一步说明 new decor 的细节内容。

(3) There were some 516,000 hotpot restaurants in the country in 2019, estimates from China's on-demand service platform Meituan showed, with the figure likely to reach 900,000 by 2022.

**翻译**:根据中国按需服务平台美团(Meituan)的估计,2019 年中国约有 51.6 万家火锅餐厅,到 2022 年,这一数字可能达到 90 万。

**分析**:some 意为"大约",该句和逗号后的内容实际为倒装,正常语序为 Estimates from China's on-demand service platform Meituan showed that there were some 516,000 hotpot restaurants in the country in 2019。作者通过倒装来突显数据,并用 with 短语进一步对其补充说明。with 短语的中心词为 figure,并用不定式短语作后置定语进一步说明"数据"的发展情况。

## Exercises

### Ⅰ. Reading and Understanding

**1. Choose the best answer to each question.**

(1) What would Xiabuxiabu do in a "worst-case scenario"?

A. Plans to turn over 800 outlets into a grocery service.

B. Provide delivery services in outlets all over China.

C. Turn the company into a fresh food delivery company.

D. Builds up e-commerce platform and serve consumers food for free.

(2) The "7-Eleven or Dingdong Maicai" mentioned in the fifth paragraph suggests that _____.

A. Xiabuxiabu can serve consumers any food they ordered

B. consumers can get a discount

C. Xiabuxiabu can serve consumers fresh meat and vegetables prepared for the hotpot

D. Xiabuxiabu can serve consumers fresh meat and vegetables prepared for the grocery store

(3) What does Xiabuxiabu do to make its own "mark"?

A. Make enough room for large groups of friends and families.

B. Launch more outlets.

C. Provide small portions and prepare one pot for each customer.

D. Provide all kinds of meat and vegetables for choice.

(4) How does Xiabuxiabu change its new stores?

A. Only change the color of the tables into white.

B. Turn the whole store into the so-called Instagram-style.

C. Change everything in the store into light grey.

D. Paint the walls into pictures that the millennials like.

(5) Which of the following choices may not correctly explain "the nimblest" in the last paragraph?

A. Xiabuxiabu builds up grocery delivery service system as a contingency plan.

B. Xiabuxiabu is changing the decor in their new stores.

C. Xiabuxiabu encourages "one person, one pot" and provides small portions.

D. Xiabuxiabu is turning parts of the outlets online to attract more consumers.

**2. Decide whether the statements are true or false.**

(1) Xiabuxiabu is renovating outlets in whole China to appeal to a young clientele.

(2) Xiabuxiabu is pushing ahead with its expansion plan to launch 1,000 outlets this year.

(3) Xiabuxiabu is abandoning its dark orange interiors in its new stores.

(4) Xiabuxiabu faces increasing competition from hotpot chains.

(5) Xiabuxiabu made a profit of 165 million yuan in 2019.

## Ⅱ. Translating the Paragraph into Chinese

Hotpot is a communal dining experience where large groups of friends and families cook plates of meat and vegetables in a soup at the centre of their table. But concerns that sharing food and gathering in confined spaces is helping to spread the coronavirus have affected the segment. Coupled with the rise of different hot pot brands, Xiabuxiabu faces many competitions and challenges. If Xiabuxiabu doesn't innovate internally and open up the situation, it will be difficult for it to stand out and become the industry leader.

## Ⅲ. Developing Critical Thinking

**Work in pairs and discuss the questions.**

(1) If you were responsible for the sales of a hotpot store, what would you do to attract more customers under the pandemic impact?

(2) Do you think food delivery service of the hotpot will be popular in the future? And why?

(3) When eating hotpot, would you prefer sharing food in a big pot with friends and families, or eating in your own pot?

扫码看答案

# Unit 5
# China's New Life

## Text A  China's "Gen Z":
## Patriotic and No Longer Looking up to the West

Exactly a century ago, young people in China fought for sweeping changes. Specifically, they wanted China, downtrodden and defeated at the turn of the 20th century, to become a modern country like the industrialized West and Japan.

The waning elites in the last days of the Qing Dynasty realized that China must "learn from the foreigners in order to beat them". And with that understanding, the first group of Chinese students set off on their overseas journeys.

The returnees brought back new ideas and knowledge. A new generation of Chinese intelligentsia was convinced that the only way to save their country from the double whammy of feudalism and colonialism was to do away with outdated Confucian thinking and adopt modern Western values, particularly science and democracy.

This New Culture Movement reached a climax on May 4, 1919 when angry students protested the violation of China's sovereignty by the *Treaty of Versailles* after World War I. It was an awakening that had profound impact on the nation's history. In a speech commemorating the centenary of the May Fourth Movement on Tuesday, Chinese President Xi Jinping hailed the movement's spirit of patriotism and called on today's youths in China to strive for national rejuvenation.

## A Newfound Confidence

If the May Fourth generation had to look to the West for answers to China's problems, it appears the tide today has changed.

For decades, U.S. foreign policy makers argued that as China opens up, more exposure to the West would lead it to embrace Western values and political system. But in fact, not only has China followed its own path, it is also rejecting the Western model exemplified by the U.S.

In 2017, the *Wall Street Journal* claimed that "Chinese exceptionalism" is the new challenge to U.S. power, saying the Chinese now see their country as ascendant and America in decline. It is a common sentiment shared by older Chinese millennials who have spent time in the West that, as the *Wall Street Journal* quoted a scholar as saying, "If you don't go abroad, you don't actually know how great China is".

Last year, a survey of young people in China jointly conducted by *China Youth Daily* and the Communist Youth League of China showed that Chinese youths possess a high degree of national identity. An overwhelming 96.1 percent of the respondents expressed that they "often feel proud of China's accomplishments," while 92.9 percent believed the country is moving in a good direction.

While these sentiments are often dismissed in the West as being "brainwashed" due to censorship, some have argued it is actually people in the West who have such a limited understanding of China through the media. On the other hand, China's tech-savvy youths today have grown up exposed to Western consumerism and popular culture, and as a result eager to know more about those countries and the outside world. Yet what they see both in the news and on the ground during travels may not be the "city on the hill" that many of their predecessors had revered.

Zak Dychtwald, CEO of Young China Group, author of *Young China: How the Restless Generation Will Change Their Country and the World*, cited China's economic miracle as a big factor in young people's national pride. "There's the sense that they don't want to westernize as they modernize. What they witness in their lifetime is this rags-to-riches story without parallel on the world stage. And they feel that exceptionalism. They are proud of that," Dychtwald said during an interview with CGTN America.

A new survey focused particularly on the "Generation Z" in China found this younger generation coming of age in the last decade expressed remarkable optimism for their own and their country's future. A significant number of those polled felt they have a responsibility to make China a strong country, something that they care personally, and a majority believe success comes from hard work.

Meanwhile, watching the unfolding of world events like Brexit, France's Yellow Vests protests, Trump presidency and the partisan fighting in the U.S. has more or less undermined confidence in some of the leading Western democracies. This by contrast reinforces the view in China that the country is doing something right.

A century after China first imported the idea of democracy, many are now wondering whether Western democracy faces a crisis at home.

## What Young People in the West Are Saying

The latest Harvard IOP Youth Poll, the most comprehensive of its kind in the U.S., found young people between the ages of 18 and 29 are experiencing anxiety, don't think older voters or elected officials care about them, and are increasingly concerned about the moral direction of the nation.

For more perspective, I asked under-30 netizens from North America and Western Europe in a small survey via social media what they think of their country and the direction it is going.

Among some 200 respondents, 67 percent felt things are getting worse in their countries. 20 percent said they wanted to emigrate or have already emigrated. Less than 10 percent believed things are getting better. Some of the chief complaints from those polled include "political divides", "corporation control", and economic and social inequalities. Others mentioned student debts and healthcare.

"The last few years everyone's been losing their minds," said Derek from the U.S. "Political divides are becoming more pronounced. The parties are polarizing themselves and demonizing each other as if we're heading to war." Jessie from Canada said even though she wouldn't want to live anywhere else, she felt that politically, things are "a mess". Seth said infrastructures in America's towns are falling apart, "Taxes are already being paid but lots of things are in shambles."

Interestingly, one user named Alexandre who moved to France from Tunisia at 18, said now things started to get better in Tunisia whereas the opposite happened in France.

It is not all doom and gloom. Serena from the U.S. said people are standing up for the rights of others including people of colors, LGBT community and women more than ever before. "It's getting better and will continue to do so," she said.

Some people also attributed these results to the ways globalized media today have shaped the views of the audiences, who tend to hear about problems all the time and take for granted the progress made. "Everyone's expectations have gone through the roof while their appreciations have fallen through the floor," one said.

**Source:**

https://news.cgtn.com/news/3d3d674d3349444e34457a6333566d54/index.html.

## Language Focus

### Useful Expressions

(1) ascendant           adj. 向上的;优越的
(2) be in shambles      混乱不堪
(3) centenary           n. 一百周年纪念
(4) demonize            v. 将……妖魔化;把……描绘成魔鬼(或危险人物等)
(5) doom and gloom      黯淡的前景
(6) downtrodden         adj. 受欺压的;被践踏的
(7) hail                v. 赞扬;称颂;跟……打招呼
(8) intelligentsia      n. 知识分子;知识阶层
(9) partisan            adj. 党派的
(10) polarize           v. 使……两极化
(11) pronounced         adj. 显著的;明确的
(12) rags-to-riches     adj. 白手起家的
(13) rejuvenation       n. 振兴;复苏

（14）savvy　　　　　　　　*adj.* 有见识的；懂实际知识的

（15）waning　　　　　　　*adj.* 衰落的；败落的

（16）whammy　　　　　　 *n.* 打击；诅咒

## Exercises

### Ⅰ. Reading and Understanding

**1. Fill in the blanks with appropriate words or expressions from the text.**

（1）The New Culture Movement reached a climax when angry students protested the violation of China's sovereignty by the *Treaty of* _____ after World War Ⅰ.

（2）For decades, U.S. foreign policy makers argued that as China opens up, it would embrace Western values and political system. But in fact, not only has China followed _____, it is also _____ the Western model exemplified by the U.S.

（3）Last year, a survey of young people in China showed that Chinese youths possess a high degree of _____.

（4）Zak Dychtwald cited China's _____ as a big factor in young people's national pride.

（5）In a small survey of young netizens from North America and Western Europe, some of their chief complaints include _____, _____ and _____.

**2. Decide whether the statements are true or false.**

（1）At the turn of the 20th century, some Chinese intellectuals believed that the only way to save China from the double whammy of feudalism and colonialism was to abandon outdated Confucian thinking and adopt modern Western values.

（2）A hundred years after China first imported the idea of democracy, many are at present in doubt whether Western democracy faces a crisis at home.

（3）A latest Harvard poll found young people in the U.S. are experiencing anxiety and increasingly concerned about the economic direction of the nation.

### Ⅱ. Translating the Paragraph into English

一项特别针对中国"Z 世代"的调查发现，在过去十年间长大成人的这一代年轻人对于他们自身的未来和国家的未来都展现出令人瞩目的乐观心态。参与调查的年轻人中,有相当一部分人认为他们有责任将中国建设成为一个强大的国家,并且大部分人相信成功来自努力工作。另一项调查显示,大多数年轻人为中国所取得的成就感到自豪,并且认为国家的发展方向是正确的。

## Ⅲ. Developing Critical Thinking

**Work in pairs and discuss the question.**

As a member of "Generation Z" in China, what do you think you can do to help make China stronger and stronger?

扫码看答案

## Text B  Twenty-Five Years of Gender Equality in China

On the occasion of the 25th anniversary of the Fourth World Conference on Women, it is of great significance to revisit the spirit of the conference and the commendable history of women's rights development in China.

In 1995, the Fourth World Conference on Women was held in Beijing. The Conference adopted the *Beijing Declaration and Platform for Action*, a programmatic document guiding efforts to promote global gender equality, put forward 12 key areas of concern for women's development, agreed on strategic objectives and a policy framework for promoting gender equality and safeguarding women's rights, and provided guidelines for action to promote gender equality around the world.

The Conference, the largest ever held by the United Nations, was an important milestone in the promotion of gender equality and women's development, and had a profound impact on the global cause of promoting women's development.

Since the convening of the Fourth World Conference on Women, significant progress has been made in promoting women's rights and development around the world, and women's living and development conditions have continued to improve. In 2015, China and UN Women jointly organized the Global Summit of Women to reaffirm their commitment to promoting gender equality and women's development and to work together for a better future.

Chinese President Xi Jinping presided over the summit and put forward four proposals on promoting gender equality and the all-round development of women. Over the past 25 years, the Chinese government has honored its commitments, upheld the spirit of the Fourth World Conference on Women in Beijing, adhered to the basic national policy on gender equality for social development and progress, continuously improved the legal system and working mechanisms for the protection of women's rights and interests, and promoted women's development in China with world-renowned achievements.

Equal participation in economic activities is an important foundation for the realization of women's all-round development. The labor force participation rate of women in China has long stayed above 60 percent, ranking first in the world. With an expanding legion of female workers and an optimized structure of women's occupations, more women are taking well-remunerated and management jobs.

In 2018, the number of female employees reached 340 million, and women accounted for 43.5 percent of all employed persons in society. Women now take 48.8 percent professional and technical jobs, 33.4 percent R&D jobs, including 54.9 percent medical and scientific R&D jobs. The percentage of female entrepreneurs in the new economy has been rising, with women accounting for 55 percent of entrepreneurs in the Internet sector. Women are actively involved in economic decision-making and management. For example, they take a quarter of leading positions in companies, up from only 10 percent in 1995.

Since 1995, China has rolled out a series of poverty alleviation plans at different stages of development, implemented the poverty reduction strategy, and made significant progress in poverty reduction. In poverty alleviation projects and actions, the emphasis has been placed on ensuring the equal participation of and benefit for poor women, leading to the significant decrease of both the number of poor women and the incidence of poverty among women. By the end of 2018, the number of poor people in rural areas nationwide had been reduced from 98.99 million in 2012 to 16.6 million, and the incidence of poverty had fallen from 10.2 percent in 2012 to 1.7 percent. About half of the people walking out of poverty were women.

The right to education is a basic human right and an important way to realize the equal development of men and women. Over the past 25 years, China has been prioritizing the development of education by promoting equal access to education and has made great headway in eliminating female illiteracy. In 2018, the illiteracy rate among the female population aged 15 and above was 7.5 percent, with a decrease of 16.6 percentage points from 1995. More and more women have gained access to higher education. In 2018, the share of female university undergraduates and junior college students as a percentage of all students on higher education reached 52.5 percent, up 17.1 percentage points from 1995. The share of females in master and doctorate programs reached 51.2 percent and 40.4 percent, up 20.6 and 24.9 percentage points from 1995, respectively.

The enjoyment of the equal right to health is essential to the well-being of women. China attaches great importance to protecting women's right to health and has continuously improved the legal and policy system for women's and children's health, by establishing a robust health service network for women and children, thereby greatly improving women's health. In 2015, women's average life expectancy was 79.4 years, with an increase of 8.9 years from 1990. The maternal mortality rate has continued to fall, from 61.9 per 100,000 in 1995 to 18.3 per 100,000 in 2018, achieving the United Nations Millennium Development Goals ahead of schedule.

It's heartening to see the achievements made in promoting women's rights in China. Nevertheless, it must be noted that there are still enormous challenges to the full realization of the development goals for women outlined in the *Beijing Declaration and Platform for Action*.

At present, discrimination against women in the job market still exists, while the level of women's participation and influence in decision-making and management still needs to be raised, and the deep-seated gender stereotype which entrenches inequality between men and women still influences people's perception and behavior to varying degrees. Going forward, we need to carry on the spirit of the Fourth World Conference on Women and make unremitting efforts to promote the all-round development of women and to build a better world for all.

**Source:**

https://news.cgtn.com/news/2020-10-02/25-years-of-gender-equality-in-China-Uf3mIZovWE/index.html.

# Language Focus

## Useful Expressions

(1) alleviation      *n.* 减轻；缓解

(2) commendable      *adj.* 值得赞扬的

(3) entrench      *v.* 使处于牢固地位；牢固确立

(4) headway      *n.* 前进；进展

(5) heartening      *adj.* 令人鼓舞的；振奋人心的

(6) incidence       *n.* 影响程度；发生率

(7) legion        *n.* 大量；大批

(8) maternal mortality rate   *n.* 孕产妇死亡率

(9) optimize        *v.* 使最优化；充分利用

(10) platform       *n.* 纲领；观点

(11) prioritize       *v.* 划分优先顺序；优先处理

(12) remunerate      *v.* 给……报酬

(13) roll out        铺开；推出

(14) unremitting      *adj.* 不懈的；持续不断的

## Exercises

### Ⅰ. Reading and Understanding

**1. Fill in the blanks with appropriate words or expressions from the text.**

(1) The Fourth World Conference on Women was held in Beijing in _____.

(2) The Conference, the largest ever held by the United Nations, was an important milestone in the promotion of _____ and women's development.

(3) _____ in economic activities is an important foundation for the realization of women's all-round development.

(4) In order to realize the equal development of men and women, _____ is a basic human right.

(5) Today, there is still _____ in the job market, while the level of _____ in decision-making and management still needs to be raised.

**2. Decide whether the statements are true or false.**

(1) The labor force participation rate of women in China has long stayed above 60 percent, ranking second in the world.

(2) Over the last 25 years, China has been prioritizing the development of education and has made great progress in getting rid of female illiteracy.

(3) The maternal mortality rate in China has continued to fall, achieving the United Nations Millennium Development Goals on time.

(4) These days, women are not actively involved in economic decision-making and management yet.

(5) Now the deep-seated gender stereotype still influences people's perception and behavior to varying degrees.

## II. Translating the Sentences into Chinese

(1) Since the convening of the Fourth World Conference on Women, significant progress has been made in promoting women's rights and development around the world, and women's living and development conditions have continued to improve.

(2) Over the past 25 years, the Chinese government has continuously improved the legal system and working mechanisms for the protection of women's rights and interests, and promoted women's development in China with world-renowned achievements.

(3) Since 1995, China has rolled out a series of poverty alleviation plans at different stages of development, implemented the poverty reduction strategy, and made significant progress in poverty reduction.

(4) With an expanding legion of female workers and an optimized structure of women's occupations, more women are taking well-remunerated and management jobs.

## III. Developing Critical Thinking

**Work in pairs and discuss the questions.**

(1) Have you ever experienced or witnessed gender discrimination in your daily life and how did you deal with it?

(2) What do you think can be done in order to enhance gender equality in China?

扫码看答案

# Unit 6
# China's New Environment

## Text A  Moving to a Green Economy

As a developing country, China seeks a sustainable way to coordinate issues related to its population, economy, society, environment, and resources. Protecting the environment and economic growth are usually regarded as contradictory. Which mechanism can make these two develop consistently? At present, the green economy has been put forward as a solution. This refers to a balanced economy that caters to the demands of environmental protection and human well-being and is aimed at harmonizing the co-existence of the economy and environment and rationally protecting resources and energy. In practice, China is still exploring the green economy construct. Setting up an ecological compensation mechanism is one of the important aspects of the green economy.

Ecological compensation mechanism is a public system, aimed at protecting the environment, boosting the harmonious coexistence of humans and nature, and utilizing administrative means and the markets to adjust the interests of the ecology's stakeholders. It just implies the polluter pays principle. In 2008, the Chinese legislature revised the *Law on the Prevention and Control of Water Pollution*, in which "ecological compensation" was first legalized in a legitimate form, closely combining environmental protection measures with the interest guarantee mechanism. This legislation directly provided a larger development space for the ecological compensation mechanism in China. Actually, before this law was enforced, China had already begun research into and practiced ecological compensation. For instance, the ecological compensation work of forest and nature reserves had achieved prominent results. Besides the forest ecological benefit compensation system, natural forests protection, returning the farmlands to forests and other ecological projects can also be regarded as compensation to ecological system degradation caused by long-term destruction.

Some of these ecological compensations have been quite successful. Returning the farmlands to forests (grasslands) is thus the largest ecological compensation practice in China in which the government invests the most. It is the first instance of China taking compensatory measures for a large-scale ecological construction project, which plays a significant role in curbing substantial ecological destruction in vulnerable areas and protecting and restoring forests and grassland resources. The pilot project of returning farmlands to forests (grasslands) started in 1999 and was completely initiated in 2002, covering 25 provinces (autonomous regions and municipalities) and more than 32,000,000 rural households in 2,279 counties of Xinjiang Uygur Autonomous Region, involving 124 million peasants and an investment of RMB 130 billion from the central government. The ecological benefits were huge. In addition, this project also solved the problem of poverty among peasants within the project regions and was welcomed by the masses. It was a win-win situation with regard to the ecology and the economy. Other large-scale ecological construction projects have kicked off in China since the 1980s, including the construction of protected forests, treatment of water loss, prevention of desertification, and protection of natural forests and the Three-river Source Area. These are significant with respect to ecological compensation—compensation for the degradation of the ecological system caused by long-term destruction. China has invested more than RMB 100 billion on these large projects. All these projects are successful practices in ecological compensation.

In addition, the arable land occupancy compensation system has been carried out in China for several years. Important ecological construction projects such as natural forest protection and fiscal subsidies for construction of nature protection regions can be viewed as compensatory. In August 2007, former State Environmental Protection General Bureau issued its *Opinion on Trial Implementation of Ecological Compensation*, which was the first directive document issued by the Chinese government on ecological compensation. The *Opinion* firstly reiterated the notion that the ecological compensation system (aimed at protecting the environment and boosting harmony between humans and nature) is the environmental economic policy whereby the interests and relationships among the stakeholders in ecological environment protection and construction are adjusted. This is done based on the service value of the ecological system, the costs of ecological protection and development, and by the means of comprehensive administrative methods and the market. The *Opinion* defined five fundamental principles for ecological compensation: the developer should protect the resources; the person who destroys the resources should restore them; the person who benefits should pay the compensation; the person who pollutes should pay for it; and the obligations, rights, and interests should be consistent. These guidelines would enhance win-win situations. The government would guide policy decisions and combine these with market control. The measures should be altered to suit local conditions, and innovations should be encouraged. In September 2007, the former State Environmental Protection General Bureau claimed to carry out the trial implementation of ecological compensation in four regions including natural reserves, important ecological function areas, mine resource development areas, and water environmental protection areas. Through trial implementation, China started to build a standardized system of ecological compensation for key areas, to explore diversified ecological compensation modes and to lay solid foundations for setting up a nationwide ecological compensation system. For ecological compensation in the river basin, local practices mainly focus on the protection of urban drinking water sources and the ecological compensation issues between upstream and downstream along medium and small water basins within administrative districts. Through these ecological compensation practices, China has gradually enriched its ecological compensation system.

However, these practices also had drawbacks because they relied on the projects, and when these projects were completed, changes occurred. This meant that ecological protection lacked continuity. Besides, it was difficult to clarify the compensation obligations in practice. Relevant authorities must continuously explore how to adjust the mechanism of government intervention in priority areas to a mechanism whereby market measures drive and sustain change.

**Source**:

Liu Junhui, Wang Jia. China's Environment[M]. Singapore:Cengage Learning Asia Pte Ltd., 2011.

 **Language Focus**

## Ⅰ. Useful Expressions

（1）administrative means　　　　　　行政手段
（2）arable land　　　　　　　　　　　耕地
（3）contradictory　　　　　　　　　　*adj.* 对立的,相互矛盾的
（4）curb　　　　　　　　　　　　　　*v.* 抑制
（5）ecological compensation mechanism　生态补偿机制
（6）kick off　　　　　　　　　　　　 开始做某事
（7）pilot project　　　　　　　　　　 试点工程
（8）returning the farmlands to forests　　退耕还林
（9）trial implementation　　　　　　　试行办法
（10）win-win situation　　　　　　　　双赢局面

## Ⅱ. Difficult Sentences

（1）Ecological compensation mechanism is a public system, aimed at protecting the environment, boosting the harmonious coexistence of humans and nature, and utilizing administrative means and the markets to adjust the interests of the ecology's stakeholders.

**翻译**:生态补偿机制是以保护环境、促进人与自然和谐共处、利用行政手段和市场调节生态利益相关者利益为目的的公共制度。

**分析**:句子的主语为 Ecological compensation mechanism；aimed 为过去分词作状语；aimed at 意为"针对"；protecting、boosting 以及 utilizing 为并列动名词结构；adjust sth. 意为"调整……以适应……"；stakeholders 意为"利益相关者"。

（2）It is the first instance of China taking compensatory measures for a large-scale ecological construction project, which plays a significant role in curbing substantial ecological destruction in vulnerable areas and protecting and restoring forests and grassland resources.

**翻译**:这是中国首次对大型生态建设项目采取补偿措施,在遏制脆弱地区实质性生态破坏、保护和恢复森林及草原资源方面发挥了重要作用。

**分析**:It 为主语;taking compensatory measures 为分词定语;China 为 taking compensatory measures 的逻辑主语;a large-scale ecological construction project 为非限定性定语从句的先行词,which 为关系代词,作从句的主语;plays a significant role 意为"发挥重要的作用";curbing substantial ecological destruction 和 protecting and restoring forests and grassland resources 为并列结构。

(3) The *Opinion* firstly reiterated the notion that the ecological compensation system (aimed at protecting the environment and boosting harmony between humans and nature) is the environmental economic policy whereby the interests and relationships among the stakeholders in ecological environment protection and construction are adjusted.

**翻译**:《意见》首先重申了生态补偿制度(以保护环境、促进人与自然和谐为目的)是调整生态环境保护和建设中各利益相关者之间利益关系的环境经济政策。

**分析**:句子的主语为 The *Opinion*;谓语为 reiterated;宾语为 the notion;that 引导的同位语从句进一步说明 the notion;从句为系表结构;whereby 为关系副词,意为"凭借",相当于 by which 引导定语从句,先行词为 policy。

 **Exercises**

Ⅰ. **Reading and Understanding**

**1. Choose the best answer to each question.**

(1) What is the end aim of green economy in China?

A. To meet the demands of environmental protection and human well-being

B. To harmonize the co-existence of the economy and environment

C. To protect the resources and energy

D. To initiate a sustainable way for the country

(2) How does China construct the ecological compensation mechanism?

A. To provide a larger development space for the ecological compensation mechanism

B. To establish a public system

C. To let the polluter pay principles

D. To begin research into and practice ecological compensation

(3) Which one is NOT brought by the arable land occupancy compensation system projects?

A. Curbing substantial ecological destruction

B. Protecting and restoring forests and grassland resources

C. Degrading the ecological system

D. Solving the problem of poverty among peasants

(4) Which one is NOT necessary to the implement of the *Opinion*?

A. The service value of the ecological system

B. Five fundamental principles

C. The costs of ecological protection and development

D. The means of comprehensive administrative methods and the market

(5) What kind of challenge will the ecological protection meet?

A. The implement of the ecological projects

B. Clarification of the compensation obligations

C. Continuity

D. Market promotion in mechanism

**2. Fill in the blanks with appropriate words or expressions from the text.**

(1) His public speeches are in direct _____ to his personal lifestyle.

(2) The damages are designed to _____ victims for their direct losses.

(3) The mayor _____ the party.

(4) We should increase input in agriculture, develop advanced technologies, _____ market speculation, increase food assistance and intensify cooperation in food.

(5) Very little has been achieved in the _____ of the peace agreement signed last January.

## Ⅱ. Translating the Paragraph into English

作为一个发展中国家,中国寻求一种可持续的方式来协调与人口、经济、社会、环境和资源有关的问题。生态补偿机制成为实现可持续发展的重要途径之一。生态补偿机制是以保护环境、促进人与自然和谐共处、利用行政手段和市场调节生态利益相关者利益为目的的公共制度。

## Ⅲ. Developing Critical Thinking

**Work in pairs and discuss the questions.**

(1) How do you value the ecological compensation system?
(2) Please talk about the actions we can take to achieve sustainable development.

扫码看答案

## Text B  Gaming the System

There are 350 million people—more than the population of the U. S.—currently taking a stand against climate change in China. But these activists are not actually taking to the streets, nor even physically planting trees. Instead, their newfound social empowerment is contained to a glowing screen open to the Alipay app, one of China's two most popular forms of electronic payment.

Alipay's foray into social engagement began with the release of the Ant Forest mobile game in 2016. Players are awarded green energy bubbles based on their real-life actions to reduce their carbon footprints, as determined by the China Beijing Environmental Exchange. These bubbles can be shared or stolen from other users and used to water a virtual tree. Once a tree matures, the points accumulated can be redeemed to plant an actual tree in a real deforested area.

Alipay's goals fit with the government's own plans to defeat deforestation, which included a "total ban" on the domestic logging industry in 2017. The "Great Green Wall" of China, a 30-year mission to plant 66 billion trees to combat the encroaching desert that already covers a quarter of China's landmass, has already seen some success. Saihanba prairie in Hebei Province, once a dusty wasteland, is now the world's largest man-made forest.

So far, over 56 million "Ant trees" have been planted by players across the country, prompting *Fortune* magazine to list Alipay's parent company, Ant Financial, sixth in its 2017 "Change the World" list. The game's image and popularity have been bolstered by innovative features. When some skeptics questioned whether Alipay was actually planting trees, the company provided access to satellite technology to monitor the growth of the forests.

In a stroke of marketing savvy, the game recently allowed groups to pool their bubbles and dedicate an "Ant tree" in honor of an ancestor, family, partner, company, or even graduating class. This is how Ms. Xiong, a 24-year-old insurance broker in Chengdu, began using the game as a part of her daily routine. She particularly liked that the frivolous fun was able to translate into something meaningful and make a difference in China's environmental problems, as well as honoring her grandfather's legacy.

Le Shen, senior public relations adviser for Ant Financial, is proud that he has already planted two trees, one for each year he has played the game. "In 2015, the smog in Beijing was terrible and people were feeling the pinch of a degraded environment," Le, one of the very first users of Ant Forest, told *The World of Chinese*. This prompted three Ant employees to start brainstorming solutions outside normal working hours.

"No one anticipated the success of the project when it first started," Le laughed, remembering that there were not even designated servers or bandwidth for the initial Ant Forest, leading to several mishaps early on.

The early success of Ant Forest can be attributed to widespread anxieties over pollution, as well as the rapid ubiquity of smart phones, broadband, and electronic payment schemes that allow Alipay to easily keep track of carbon-offsetting activities. Users can boost up on green energy bubbles by walking or using dockless bikes. Additionally, shoppers can reduce carbon emissions by making daily transactions (household utilities, subway tickets, or groceries) with their bank-account linked app.

While reducing the number of four-inch receipts and ticket stubs might not seem world-changing behavior, Le believes that, through economies of scale, "just the smallest change of behavior can have a huge impact."

It should come as no surprise that almost all these green energy activities incentivize the use of Alipay's payment platform. Indeed, since the introduction of Ant Forest, users are spending substantially more time on the app—giving Alipay an edge over its social media-driven rival, WeChat Wallet. However, Ant Financial's commercial interests are exactly what make the project both sustainable and relevant to the future of humankind, says Simon Zadek, co-director of the United Nations Environment Programs (UNEP) Inquiry into the Design of a Sustainable Financial System.

Under Zadek's leadership, the UNEP partnered with Ant Forest just a month after its release, noting that "historically, the United Nations' engagement has been with governments. In the 21st century. We have realized that this government focus has its limits and to bring about change. We must harvest other mechanisms of engagement, especially inside the market with the digital world."

Alipay's 520 million users illustrate the growing power of Chinese companies. Zadek recently founded the "Sustainable Digital Finance Alliance" with Ant Financial, the first global public-private partnership with a private Chinese company. He hopes the platform will address worldwide social welfare, especially in Ant Financials overseas investments such as India's Paytm online payment platform.

Private companies like Alipay have been the impetus of China's recent economic growth, engraining themselves in people's daily life by tapping into their needs and motivations. One reason for Ant Forest's success, as Zadek hypothesizes to *The World of Chinese*, was that it met a need in society, giving young people the chance to make a social difference outside of a closed political sphere. The numbers back him up—an estimated 65 percent of Ant Forest users are under 28. It is yet to be seen, however, how the government will engage with the growing financial and social power of these non-state-owned companies.

Asked about future challenges of Ant Forest, Le ducked concerns about increased government oversight, and instead half-way joked, "Quite honestly, we are soon going to run out of places to plant trees."

**Source:**

http://www.theworldofchinese.com/2018/10/gaming-the-system/.

# Language Focus

## I. Useful Expressions

| | | |
|---|---|---|
| (1) bolster | *v.* | 改善 |
| (2) frivolous | *adj.* | 琐碎的，无用的 |
| (3) impetus | *n.* | 动力 |
| (4) incentivize | *v.* | 以物质激励 |
| (5) man-made forest | | 人造林 |
| (6) non-state-owned | *adj.* | 非国有的 |
| (7) prairie | *n.* | 草原 |

（8）redeem　　　　　　　vt. 兑换

（9）skeptic　　　　　　　n. 怀疑论者

（10）stub　　　　　　　　n.［会计］存根

## Ⅱ. Difficult Sentences

（1）Players are awarded green energy bubbles based on their real-life actions to reduce their carbon footprints, as determined by the China Beijing Environmental Exchange.

**翻译：**根据中国北京环境交易所的决定，玩家在现实生活中为减少碳排放而采取的行动将被给予绿色能量泡泡。

**分析：**该句子的主干结构为 Players are awarded bubbles；过去分词短语 based on 意为"以……为依据"，作方式状语；to reduce their carbon footprints 为不定式作目的状语；as determined by the China Beijing Environmental Exchange 为宾语补足语。

（2）The early success of Ant Forest can be attributed to widespread anxieties over pollution, as well as the rapid ubiquity of smart phones, broadband, and electronic payment schemes that allow Alipay to easily keep track of carbon-offsetting activities.

**翻译：**蚂蚁森林的早期成功可以归因于对污染的广泛担忧，以及智能手机、宽带和电子支付计划的迅速普及，这些计划使支付宝能够轻松记录碳抵消活动。

**分析：**该句主干结构为 The success can be attribute to anxieties；over pollution 为介词短语作宾语补足语；as well as 表示"除……之外（也）"，介词短语作宾语补足语表示并列；that 引导限制性定语从句，先行词为 schemes，在从句中作主语；keep track of 意为"跟踪、记录"；carbon-offsetting activities 意为"碳抵消活动"。

（3）One reason for Ant Forest's success, as Zadek hypothesizes to *The World of Chinese*, was that it met a need in society, giving young people the chance to make a social difference outside of a closed political sphere.

**翻译：**扎德克向《汉语世界》假设，蚂蚁森林成功的一个原因是它满足了社会的需求，使年轻人有机会在封闭的政治领域之外做出改变。

**分析：**该句子主干为主系表结构。One reason for Ant Forest's success, as Zadek hypothesizes to *The World of Chinese* 是一个省略了关系代词 that 的定语从

句，先行词为 reason，作从句中的宾语；第二个 that 引导的从句作表语，that 不作任何成分；giving 引导的内容是现在分词作伴随状语，give sb. sth. 意为"给予某人某物"。

 **Exercises**

Ⅰ. Reading and Understanding

**1. Choose the best answer to each question.**

(1) How do the environmental activists do to take a stand against the climate in China?

　A. To focus on a glowing screen

　B. To open the Alipay App

　C. To plant trees

　D. To make the use of Ant Forest

(2) What can the users do with the bubbles?

　A. They can steal the bubbles from their friends.

　B. They can use the bubbles to water a virtual tree.

　C. They can share the bubbles with other users.

　D. All of above

(3) Why do the users take delight in the Ant Forest game?

　A. Because the game can bring them much fun

　B. Because they can get the significances of the game

　C. Because they are used to play the game

　D. Because they can commemorate their legacy

(4) How does Alipay keep the Ant Forest project sustainable?

　A. To gather more energy bubbles

　B. To reduce carbon emissions

C. To encourage people to use Alipay's payment platform

D. To rely on the commercial interests

(5) What kind of challenge will the Ant Financial face?

A. There is no place to plant the trees.

B. The users will lose interests.

C. The government's engagement will increase.

D. WeChat Wallet will be more competitive.

**2. Fill in the blanks with appropriate words or expressions from the text.**

(1) The group says it wants politicians to stop wasting public money on what it believes are _____ projects.

(2) These companies are all vying for your business; here is why only those who _____ their offer with rewards should be considered.

(3) This voucher can be _____ at any of our branches.

(4) Hopes of an early cut in interest rates _____ confidence.

(5) It includes the enterprises that are held by society, collectivity, individual, private sectors, pool and _____ power.

## Ⅱ. Developing Critical Thinking

**Work in pairs and discuss the questions.**

(1) Do you play the Ant Forest? How do you think of the way that Ant Financial takes?

(2) How do you think about the future of Ant Forest under the government's tight oversight?

扫码看答案

# Unit 7
# China's New Education

## Text A  New Era of Education in China

China has the largest education system in the world. In July 2020, there were 10.71 million students taking the National Higher Education Entrance Examination (Gao Kao) in China. Investment in education accounts for about 4% of total GDP in China. In 1986, the Chinese government passed a compulsory education law, making nine years of education mandatory for all Chinese children. Today, the Ministry of Education estimates that above 99 percent of the school-age children have received universal nine-year basic education.

On April 2019, Ministry of Education of the People's Republic of China announced a total of 492,185 international students were studying in China in 2018. International students have enrolled in over 1,004 higher education institutions in China. China has a long history of providing education to international students studying in high schools and universities in China. Over the past few years, the number of international students who study abroad in China has significantly increased every year.

The higher education sector has growth as well. China has increased the proportion of its college-age population in higher education to over 20 percent now from 1.4 percent in 1978. At the same time, China is improving the quality of education through a major effort at school curriculum reform.

China has a consistent teacher development system. Teaching has historically been and remains today a highly respected profession in China. Teachers have strong preparation in their subject matter and prospective teachers spend a great deal of time observing the classrooms of experienced teachers, often in schools attached to their universities. Once teachers are employed in school, there is a system of induction and continuous professional development in which groups of teachers work together with master teachers on lesson plans and improvement.

## Development of MOOCs in China

Massive open online courses (MOOCs), allowing anyone, anywhere to engage in higher education, have taken off in China as the country embraces distance learning. MOOCs started to become popular in China in 2013, and the courses often benefit those living in remote areas.

The Ministry of Education said there are more than 10 MOOC platforms in China, and over 460 universities and colleges have introduced more than 3,200 online courses through those platforms, with more than 55 million viewers. Meanwhile, over 200 Chinese online courses have joined international MOOC platforms, winning a reputation across the world. The Ministry of Education also introduced 490 "elaborate online courses" earlier on Monday, which represent the highest level of open online courses in China. Around 70 percent of the courses are provided by China's top universities, including Peking University, Tsinghua University and Wuhan University.

However, creating more MOOCs in China creates its own set of challenges. Experts believe that the quality of online courses needs to improve, and that different universities should develop diverse courses with their own characteristics. Teachers also need to be trained to adjust their teaching methods to adapt to online education, and the interaction between teachers and students should be strengthened. Experts have also urged education departments to set strict standards to ensure and monitor the qualifications of MOOC platforms.

## New Challenge of Online Education amid Pandemic

The private sector for education in China has been adversely affected by the COVID-19 outbreak, arousing extensive societal attention and discussion. The outbreak has had a tremendous and profound impact on the market's landscape and dynamics.

First, all educational institutions, from public schools to after-school tutoring centers, have either delayed recommencement or switched to online learning. Traditional offline tutoring institutions have been suffering from a cash flow shortage—a lot of clients have demanded refunds since the classes were disrupted. On the other hand, downloads of online tutoring apps soared five to 30 times the numbers seen before the outbreak.

We estimate that China's private education industry will witness negative growth in 2020. While private school education providers will remain stable due to resilient demand, training businesses, such as after-school tutoring, English language teaching and vocational training, as well as the experience-based education segment, which includes educational tours and early-years learning centers, will suffer a serious economic blow due to social distancing initiatives.

Conversely, the adoption of online education will accelerate. Having online classes has been the main solution for schools and tutoring institutions amid the outbreak. Some online tutoring apps have leveraged this opportunity to attract students by offering free or low-cost classes, leading to a surge in online education user numbers and adoption rates. According to Oliver Wyman, the market for China's online after-school tutoring was 20 billion RMB ($2.8 billion) in 2019. Companies offering online solutions to schools and offline training providers also benefited from this exponentially growing demand for online education.

China's training businesses (e.g., tutoring, test preparation, English language lessons, vocational training) have primarily adopted offline delivery models. During the COVID-19 outbreak, offline players have tried online delivery to offset the effects of both the outbreak and its associated regulatory impacts, while existing online players have leveraged free or low-cost classes to attract trial customers.

Leading Chinese online training providers have all reported more than 20 million new users during the second half of February. However, with a lot of customer overlap among competitors and low attendance rates, the quality of the trial users is relatively low. Thus, the conversion rate to full-fee paying users likely will not be as encouraging as expected. Nevertheless, online education is a growing trend, and customer acquisition costs should fall drastically in the short term.

## Industry Competition and Consolidation

There will be a widening competition gap between the leading and lagging offline training providers. We believe the leading players, with their online product capabilities and agile long-tail operations, will survive during this period. However, we believe that over 70% of medium- and small-sized offline operators—which will only likely return to operation in mid-to-late May—will face a severe cash flow shortage, and nearly half of them may have to close. The circumstances should create a great opportunity for the industry consolidation.

In terms of online competition, the leading players will gain further domination in the market. Large online classes are the mainstream product right now, and they also offer the best economic model at present in terms of scalability and profitability. Interestingly, the current competition landscape still focuses on the respective players' customer acquisition, conversion and retention capabilities. Product differentiation is not a priority at this stage. In the after-school tutoring segment, we believe that it will be very difficult for any late-comers to gain a significant market share from the current market leaders.

After the coronavirus outbreak subsides, we believe that the leading offline providers and some of the medium- and small-sized ones will keep offering online courses as a supplement or tool to attract new customers. We also expect that online-merge-offline delivery, a blended learning solution that connects online and offline venue, content, teaching or services, will emerge as one of the key delivery models in the long run.

China's Ministry of Education has launched an initiative to ensure learning is not disrupted to encourage all schools to leverage online platforms to continue teaching. We believe that some countries with severe outbreaks may adopt similar online learning approaches, especially in the degree education sector.

Besides the collaboration tools that are already in place, educational tool providers are also playing an important role in providing both the public education system and private tutoring businesses with online resources to facilitate teaching, such as live streaming platforms, video conferencing, chatting rooms and online tests.

This segment consists of not only internet giants, but also educational sector specialists. With their large customer base and online traffic advantage, the internet giants already enjoy half of the market share and plan to build their own educational ecosystems. Vertical specialists have leveraged their strong track record in the education industry, as well as their comprehensive understanding of customer demands, to also enjoy a 50% market share.

## Post-COVID-19

Content providers have advanced side-by-side and acquired many new customers. These customers are mostly medium- and small-sized training providers with relatively weaker teaching and operational capabilities. As such, they need support in terms of not only technology and tools, but content as well. We expect that the active user ratio for both schools and training providers will decrease after the COVID-19 outbreak subsides and the delivery model shifts back to offline. The lingering question, then, for these businesses is how best to add more modules and other content online to increase customer stickiness.

**Source:**

[1] https://www.chinaeducenter.com/en/cedu.php.

[2] https://news.cgtn.com/news/2020-10-10/China-s-online-education-industry-witnessing-golden-age--UtGZJ0fEpG/index.html.

[3] https://news.cgtn.com/news/7955444f79677a6333566d54/index.html.

# Language Focus

## I. Useful Expressions

(1) consistent            adj. 一致的;始终如一的
(2) continuous            adj. 不断的;持续的;连续的
(3) enroll in             入学,注册
(4) landscape             n. 局面
(5) monitor               v. 监视;检查;跟踪调查

(6) remote　　　　　　　　　　　　*adj.* 偏远的；偏僻的

(7) reputation　　　　　　　　　　*n.* 名誉；名声

(8) resilient　　　　　　　　　　　*adj.* 可迅速恢复的；有适应力的

(9) shift back　　　　　　　　　　后移，回退

(10) urge　　　　　　　　　　　　*v.* 敦促；催促；力劝

## Ⅱ. Difficult Sentences

(1) Traditional offline tutoring institutions have been suffering from a cash flow shortage—a lot of clients have demanded refunds since the classes were disrupted.

**翻译**：传统的线下培训机构经历着艰难的现金流缺失窘况——由于课程中断，大部分客户要求退款。

**分析**：本句前半句使用了现在完成进行时时态，通过使用 have been suffering from 表示过去到现在持续一段时间内的事态发生情况和变化，同时带有一种较为强烈的焦急、担忧的情感，比单纯使用现在完成时更富有情绪张力。后半句则使用现在完成时 have demanded，强调过去对现在的某种影响，态度较为客观谨慎。该句在时态使用方面，相较上下文语境非常严谨，是写作中应当模仿和学习的经典结构。

(2) While private school education providers will remain stable due to resilient demand, training businesses, such as after-school tutoring, English language teaching and vocational training, as well as the experience-based education segment, which includes educational tours and early-years learning centers, will suffer a serious economic blow due to social distancing initiatives.

**翻译**：私立学校教育机构的培训业务，如课后辅导、英语教学和职业培训等，由于弹性需求，仍能够保持稳定的服务。但一些以体验为主的教育业务，如游学教育、早教中心等，由于疫情期间的社会隔离现状，仍将经历严峻的经济难关和挑战。

**分析**：While 引导了一个让步状语从句，指出疫情期间由于隔离等政策的实施，一些线下教育机构所面临的挑战和难关。在理解本句时，需注意 While 后面引导的从句表达了一种让步含义，在翻译时需要把转折的逻辑意义体现出来。全句较长，在理解上应当厘清句子主旨，把握全句语义重点。

（3）Some online tutoring apps have leveraged this opportunity to attract students by offering free or low-cost classes, leading to a surge in online education user numbers and adoption rates.

**翻译**：一些在线辅导应用利用这个机会，通过提供免费或低成本的课程来吸引学生，使在线教育用户数量和使用频率猛增。

**分析**：本句中 leverage 一词用得非常传神，leverage 本意为"利用，施加杠杆"，相较使用 utilize 等词更为形象生动，体现了在特殊的疫情时期，一些在线教育机构把握时机，大力推出免费课程的手段和商业策略。leading 引出此行为的结果，通过言简意赅的手法直接引出后半句的结论，整个句子非常通顺凝练，值得进行仿写练习。

（4）Thus, the conversion rate to full-fee paying users likely will not be as encouraging as expected. Nevertheless, online education is a growing trend, and customer acquisition costs should fall drastically in the short term.

**翻译**：因此，完全付费用户的转化率可能不会像预期的那么令人满意。然而，在线教育有一个不断增长的趋势，短期内获取客户的成本会大幅下降。

**分析**：本句中通过使用逻辑连接词 nevertheless 表达了两句间转折的逻辑关系。正确使用逻辑连接词是学术写作或新闻写作的重要技能。句子与句子之间的逻辑架构，可通过选择不同的逻辑连接词实现具体化。同时，本句中时态多变，体现了不同的语境效果，值得思考、模仿。

# Exercises

## Ⅰ. Reading and Understanding

**Choose the best answer to each question.**

（1）Which is the best word to describe development of online education amid pandemic period in China?

A. Sluggish

B. Moderate

C. Vigorous

D. Unenlightened

(2) According to the passage, massive open online courses will chiefly benefit _____.

A. students who are living in remote lessons or online courses

B. students who are studying in university by off-line teaching activities

C. students who are acquiring knowledge in those training institutions locally

D. students who are not familiars with MOOC platforms

(3) Which of the following is NOT a perceived advantage of online education affected by the COVID-19?

A. Free fee

B. Low cost

C. Large size

D. Differentiation

(4) Which of the following idea is NOT cited in the passage?

A. China contains the largest scale education system in the world.

B. China has potential capability in attracting huge number of international student recent years.

C. MOOCs is particularly prevalent more than 20 years among higher education.

D. Teacher development system is well supported in Chinese universities.

(5) According to the passage, in China, the aspects for MOOCs improvement can be assumed EXCEPT _____.

A. quality of teaching in online courses

B. teachers' training and their academic development

C. teaching methodology and class interaction

D. quantity and gross number of online courses

## II. Dealing with Unfamiliar Words

**Please match the words with their meanings.**

| A | B |
|---|---|
| (1) estimate | a. mutual action or influence |
| (2) curriculum | b. to form an idea of the cost, size, value, etc. |
| (3) embrace | c. the process of uniting the quality of being untied |
| (4) interaction | d. the subjects that are included in a course of a school, college, etc. |
| (5) disrupt | e. in an exponential manner |
| (6) exponentially | f. to make it difficult in the normal way |
| (7) consolidation | g. to accept an idea, a proposal, a set of beliefs, etc. |

## III. Translating the Paragraph into English

为了应对新冠肺炎疫情,中国所有的大学将春季学期全部课程转移到网上,108万教师制作了110万个在线课程,此举也为推动在线教育和慕课的创新发展奠定了坚实的基础。慕课和在线教育的独特优势得以被充分利用,来推动教育公平及优质教育资源共享,实现人人皆学、处处能学、时时可学。

## IV. Developing Critical Thinking

**Work in pairs and discuss the questions.**

(1) What's your own experience of taking online education during the period of COVID-19?

(2) What's your own opinion on online course development in China?

(3) What's your suggestion for further improvement of online education for higher education?

扫码看答案

# Text B  The COVID-19 Pandemic Has Changed Education Forever

While countries are at different points in their COVID-19 infection rates, worldwide there are currently more than 1.2 billion children in 186 countries affected by school closures due to the pandemic. In Denmark, children up to the age of 11 are returning to nurseries and schools after initially closing on 12 March, but in South Korea, students are responding to roll calls from their teachers online. With this sudden shift away from the classroom in many parts of the globe, some are wondering whether the adoption of online learning will continue to persist post-pandemic, and how such a shift would impact the worldwide education market.

Even before COVID-19, there was already high growth and adoption in education technology, with global edtech investments reaching US $18.66 billion in 2019 and the overall market for online education projected to reach $350 billion by 2025. Whether it is language apps, virtual tutoring, video conferencing tools, or online learning software, there has been a significant surge in usage since COVID-19.

## How Is the Education Sector Responding to COVID-19?

In response to significant demand, many online learning platforms are offering free access to their services, including platforms like BYJU's, a Bangalore-based educational technology and online tutoring firm founded in 2011, which is now the world's most highly valued edtech company. Since announcing free live classes on its Think & Learn app, BYJU's has seen a 200% increase in the number of new students using its product, according to Mrinal Mohit, the company's Chief Operating Officer.

Tencent classroom, meanwhile, has been used extensively since mid-February after the Chinese government instructed a quarter of a billion full-time students to resume their studies through online platforms. This resulted in the largest "online movement" in the history of education with approximately 730,000, or 81% of K-12 students, attending classes via the Tencent K-12 Online School in Wuhan.

Other companies are bolstering capabilities to provide a one-stop shop for teachers and students. For example, Lark, a Singapore-based collaboration suite initially developed by ByteDance as an internal tool to meet its own exponential growth, began offering teachers and students unlimited video conferencing time, auto-translation capabilities, real-time co-editing of project work, and smart calendar scheduling, amongst other features. To do so quickly and in a time of crisis, Lark ramped up its global server infrastructure and engineering capabilities to ensure reliable connectivity.

Alibaba's distance learning solution, DingTalk, had to prepare for a similar influx, "To support large-scale remote work, the platform tapped Alibaba Cloud to deploy more than 100,000 new cloud servers in just two hours last month—setting a new record for rapid capacity expansion," according to DingTalk CEO, Chen Hang.

Some school districts are forming unique partnerships, like the one between The Los Angeles Unified School District and PBS SoCal/KCET to offer local educational broadcasts, with separate channels focused on different ages, and a range of digital options. Media organizations are also powering virtual learning; Bitesize Daily, launched on 20 April, is offering 14 weeks of curriculum-based learning for kids across the UK with celebrities like Manchester City footballer Sergio Aguero teaching some of the content.

## What Does This Mean for the Future of Learning?

While some believe that the unplanned and rapid move to online learning—with no training, insufficient bandwidth, and little preparation—will results in a poor user experience that is unconducive to sustained growth, others believe that a new hybrid model of education will emerge, with significant benefits. "I believe that the integration of information technology in education will be further accelerated and that online education will eventually become an integral component of school education," says Wang Tao, Vice President of Tencent Cloud and Vice President of Tencent Education.

There have already been successful transitions amongst many universities. For example, Zhejiang University managed to get more than 5,000 courses online just two weeks into the transition using "DingTalk ZJU". The Imperial College London started offering a course on the science of coronavirus, which is now the most enrolled class launched in 2020 on Coursera.

Many are already touting the benefits. Dr Amjad, a professor at The University of Jordan who has been using Lark to teach his students says, "It has changed the way of teaching. It enables me to reach out to my students more efficiently and effectively through chat groups, video meetings, voting and also document sharing, especially during this pandemic. My students also find it is easier to communicate on Lark. I will stick to Lark even after coronavirus. I believe traditional offline learning and e-learning can go hand by hand."

## The Challenges of Online Learning

There are, however, challenges to overcome. Some students without reliable internet access and/or technology struggle to participate in digital learning; this gap is seen across countries and between income brackets within countries. For example, whilst 95% of students in Switzerland, Norway, and Austria have a computer to use for their schoolwork, only 34% in Indonesia do, according to OECD data.

In the US, there is a significant gap between those from privileged and disadvantaged backgrounds: whilst virtually all 15-year-olds from a privileged background said they had a computer to work on, nearly 25% of those from disadvantaged backgrounds did not. While some schools and governments have been providing digital equipment to students in need, such as in New South Wales, Australia, many are still concerned that the pandemic will widen the digital divide.

## Is Learning Online as Effective?

For those who do have access to the right technology, there is evidence that learning online can be more effective in a number of ways. Some research shows that on average, students retain 25%~60% more material when learning online compared to only 8%~10% in a classroom. This is mostly due to the students being able to learn faster online. E-learning requires 40%~60% less time to learn than in a traditional classroom setting because students can learn at their own pace, going back and re-reading, skipping, or accelerating through concepts as they choose.

Nevertheless, the effectiveness of online learning varies amongst age groups. The general consensus on children, especially younger ones, is that a structured environment is required, because kids are more easily distracted. To get the full benefit of online learning, there needs to be a concerted effort to provide this structure and go beyond replicating a physical class/lecture through video capabilities, instead of using a range of collaboration tools and engagement methods that promote "inclusion, personalization and intelligence", according to Dowson Tong, Senior Executive Vice President of Tencent and President of its Cloud and Smart Industries Group.

Studies have shown that children extensively use their senses to learn, making learning funny and effective through the use of technology, according to BYJU's Mrinal Mohit. "Over a period, we have observed that clever integration of games has demonstrated higher engagement and increased motivation towards learning especially among younger students, making them truly fall in love with learning," he says.

### A Changing Education Imperative

It is clear that this pandemic has utterly disrupted an education system that many asserts were already losing its relevance. In his book, *21 Lessons for the 21st Century*, scholar Yuval Noah Harari outlines how schools continue to focus on traditional academic skills and rote learning, rather than on skills such as critical thinking and adaptability, which will be more important for success in the future. Could the move to online learning be the catalyst to create a new, more effective method of educating students? While some worry that the hasty nature of the transition online may have hindered this goal, others plan to make e-learning part of their "new normal" after experiencing the benefits first-hand.

### The Importance of Disseminating Knowledge Is Highlighted through COVID-19

Major world events are often an inflection point for rapid innovation—a clear example is the rise of e-commerce post-SARS. While we have yet to see whether this will apply to e-learning post-COVID-19, it is one of the few sectors where investment has not dried up. What has been made clear through this pandemic is the importance of disseminating knowledge across borders, companies, and all parts of society. If online learning technology can play a role here, it is incumbent upon all of us to explore its full potential.

**Source**:

https://www.weforum.org/agenda/2020/04/coronavirus-education-global-covid19-online-digital-learning/.

## Language Focus

### Ⅰ. Useful Expressions

(1) adaptability　　　　　　　　*n.* 适应性

(2) bandwidth　　　　　　　　　*n.* 带宽;频宽

(3) consensus　　　　　　　　　*n.* 一致的意见,共识,舆论

(4) disseminating　　　　　　　*adj.* 散布的,传播的

(5) hasty　　　　　　　　　　　*adj.* 仓促的,匆忙的

(6) incumbent　　　　　　　　　*adj.* 在职的,现任的

(7) infrastructure　　　　　　　*n.* (国家或机构的)基础设施,基础建设

(8) integration　　　　　　　　 *n.* 一体化,集合

(9) resume　　　　　　　　　　*v.* 重新开始,继续

### Ⅱ. Difficult Sentences

(1) While some believe that the unplanned and rapid move to online learning—with no training, insufficient bandwidth, and little preparation—will results in a poor user experience that is unconducive to sustained growth, others believe that a new hybrid model of education will emerge, with significant benefits.

**翻译**:有些人认为,无计划性、过快转向在线学习(没有培训、带宽不足、准备不充分)将导致用户体验不佳,不利于在线学习持续发展。而另一些人则认为,一种新的混合教育模式将会蓬勃发展,并带来显著的好处。

**分析**:本句是由 While 引导的让步状语从句,逻辑上表示转折。句中的 with no training, insufficient bandwidth, and little preparation 为插入语,巧妙地将较长的

句子进行了适度隔断,读起来朗朗上口,附加语言信息也较为丰富充分,是值得仿写的写作句型。

(2) Nevertheless, the effectiveness of online learning varies amongst age groups. The general consensus on children, especially younger ones, is that a structured environment is required, because kids are more easily distracted.

**翻译**:尽管如此,对于不同年龄段的孩子,在线学习的有效性有所不同。人们普遍认为孩子,尤其年龄更小的孩子,需要一个更规范的环境,因为他们更容易分心。

**分析**:本句中逻辑连接词 Nevertheless 表示让步,意为"尽管……",后半句中 especially 为副词,往往引导需要强调的结构,位于主语和谓语之间,以实现强调语义的目,译为"尤其年龄更小的孩子"。使用副词引导的插入语作为强调结构,是高级英语写作中常使用的手法。

(3) Over a period, we have observed that clever integration of games has demonstrated higher engagement and increased motivation towards learning especially among younger students, making them truly fall in love with learning.

**翻译**:一段时间以来,我们观察到,巧妙整合设计的游戏,会提高学生的参与度,增强学习动机,尤其能使年龄更小的学生真正爱上学习。

**分析**:本句中 has demonstrated 和 increased 作为并列谓语动词出现。英文句子中的并列结构往往需要语法结构上的平衡,比如,两个并列动词需要使用同一时态,不可时态混乱,此句中 increased 前省略了一个 has,这一点值得注意。

(4) While some worry that the hasty nature of the transition online may have hindered this goal, others plan to make e-learning part of their "new normal" after experiencing the benefits first-hand.

**翻译**:虽然有些人担心过于草率地过渡到在线学习,可能阻碍了这一目标的实现,但也有人计划在亲身体验到这些好处之后,让电子学习成为他们"新常态"的一部分。

**分析**:本句中 hinder 一词表示"阻碍,阻止"。常用于 hinder sb./sth. (from sth./from doing sth.)这样的结构。句中 first-hand 表示"一手的,直接的",也可引申为"亲身,亲自"的含义。

(5) What has been made clear through this pandemic is the importance of disseminating knowledge across borders, companies, and all parts of society.

**翻译**：通过这次疫情的爆发，人们清楚地认识到了跨国界、跨公司和跨社会各方面传播知识的重要性。

**分析**：本句中 What has been made clear through this pandemic 为主语从句，注意汉语翻译需要重新调整语序，以适应中文语言表达习惯。在英汉阅读理解以及翻译实操过程中，往往需要注意从句语序的调整问题。尤其是复杂句长难句的理解与翻译，更需要调整语序，完成句子结构的汉英转化。

# Exercises

## Ⅰ. Reading and Understanding

**Choose the best answer to each question.**

(1) The first paragraph is mainly about _____.

A. how many people were infected by COVID-19 in Denmark and South Korea

B. why most nurseries and schools closed on 12 March

C. current alteration of education methods and platform in different countries amongst COVID-19

D. the effects of COVID-19 on students' health and routine

(2) The author sees online learning is effective because _____.

A. most students acquired more learning material compared to offline class

B. learning efficiency through Internet is much better than in classroom

C. online learning saves more money

D. students may accept a self-adapting learning method in virtual classroom

(3) The main reason that the COVID-19 has suddenly switched traditional education approach is due to _____.

A. epidemic spread all over the world

B. scientific and technological advancement in remote education

C. adoption for both student and teacher of online learning

D. all above choices

(4) What is the author's attitude towards online education development?

A. Repugnant

B. Positive

C. Skeptical

D. Rejective

(5) The author believes that the challenges of online learning are EXCEPT _____.

A. the acceptability of online classroom

B. unreliable internet access and undeveloped virtual technology

C. insufficient or lacking terminal equipment

D. unbalance economic condition between different countries

## II. Dealing with Unfamiliar Words

**Please complete the following sentences with listed words. Change the form where necessary.**

| exponential   investment   collaboration   adoption   bolstering   deploy   hybrid   accelerated   hindered   accelerate   infection |
|---|

(1) It is not possible to _____ another person through shaking hands.

(2) The council is expected to _____ the new policy at its next meeting.

(3) Further investigation was _____ by the loss of all documentation on the case.

(4) The project has demanded considerable _____ of time and effort.

(5) The country is free to adopt policies to _____ its economy.

(6) The government worked in close _____ with teachers on the new curriculum.

(7) The quantity of chemical pollutants has increased _____.

(8) The president said he had no intention of _____ ground troops.

(9) All these brightly colored _____ are so lovely in the garden.

(10) Growth will _____ to 2.9 percent next year.

## III. Translating the Following Sentences into Chinese

(1) Whether it is language apps, virtual tutoring, video conferencing tools, or online learning software, there has been a significant surge in usage since COVID-19.

_____

_____

(2) Tencent classroom, meanwhile, has been used extensively since mid-February after the Chinese government instructed a quarter of a billion full-time students to resume their studies through online platforms.

_____

_____

(3) For those who do have access to the right technology, there is evidence that learning online can be more effective in a number of ways.

_____

_____

(4) It is clear that this pandemic has utterly disrupted an education system that many asserts were already losing its relevance.

_____

_____

## IV. Developing Critical Thinking

**Work in pairs and discuss the questions.**

(1) Why the author said that "if online learning technology can play a role here, it is incumbent upon all of us to explore its full potential" at end of the passage?

(2) What can you learn about online technology role from this passage compared to traditional education approach?

(3) What's your own experience about online classroom? Discuss the advantages or disadvantages you may offer.

扫码看答案

# Unit 8
# China's New Economy

## Text A  China's Growth Gives Confidence to World Economy

The past three months in China have shown what can be achieved if the pandemic is brought under control: China's GDP in the third quarter grew 4.9 percent compared with the previous year, showing that the economy is on a solid track to the pre-pandemic levels.

The growth rate fell short of the expectation of 5.2~5.5 percent, but it is still a remarkable achievement considering other countries are still struggling with the pandemic and climbing out of the economic mire. Even though major economies are expecting a growth in the third quarter, the chance of going back to pre-pandemic levels is slim, as the second wave of COVID-19 is already on the way.

The figure also confirms the latest forecast from the IMF that China will be the only major economy that grows this year at 1.9 percent, while U.S. economy is projected to shrink by 4.3 percent and Eurozone by 8.3 percent.

"It's an encouraging and hopeful message for the rest of the world," said Rob Subbaraman, global head of macro research at Nomura Holdings Inc. in Singapore in a Bloomberg interview. "If you successfully handle the health crisis, your economy can recover."

The world may look enviously at China's economic recovery, but its recovery path has been hard to replicate for other countries: a complete shutdown first to stop local transmission and then gradual reopening of all industries. There were some small clusters of COVID-19 cases, but they were also brought to control swiftly, with quick government actions to trace contacts and carry out testing at a large scale.

The signs are promising. In the second quarter, only the farming sector grew, but in the third quarter, both industry and service sectors started to recover as well. This means that people are having more time spending. The first three quarters have seen a 15.3-percent growth in online retail sales.

"China will be the key driver of global growth" in 2020 and 2021, said Eswar Prasad, former head of the IMF's China division, according to an article in the *Wall Street Journal*.

China's contributions to the world economy are more than just GDP numbers. In a highly globalized world, its recovery will also have spillover effect on other countries. Chinese consumers are spending, and they are spending big, even for luxury goods. The retail sales of the world's largest luxury goods company, LVMH, have grown 13 percent on a year-on-year basis in its Asia market, the only growth from all its markets around the world.

Catering businesses around the world have suffered the most from the pandemic. According to *Wall Street Journal*, Domino's Pizza Inc. is closing 300 stores around the world due to the coronavirus. But the strong retail sales growth in China have "offered a lifeline" to the piazza marker. Its Chief Executive Richard Allision calls China "a terrific success story in 2020".

There is a concern that China's growth was mainly driven by exports of medical equipment to other countries. Data from the third quarter does show that imports have not resumed to pre-pandemic levels. But in September alone, imports increased 13.2 percent, becoming a stabilizing factor for global industrial and supply chains. And the supply of masks from China means countries battling against the coronavirus can buy a large bulk of masks and protective suits quickly and at an affordable price. The first seven months of this year saw an almost 400-percent increase in American imports of epidemic-prevention products from China.

In the meantime, China is also buying more iron ore from Brazil, more soybeans and pork from the U.S., and more palm oil from Malaysia. According to *The New York Times*, this has also partly reversed the steep drop in commodity prices during the first quarter and eased the pandemic's impact on certain industries.

China's economy is expected to continue to pick up in the fourth quarter and retain its position as the main engine of global economic growth. Do uncertainties still exist? Sure. But in this bleak situation, China's growth is still the brightest silver lining for global economy.

**Source:**

https://news.cgtn.com/news/2020-10-20/China-s-growth-gives-confidence-to-world-economy-UKfQvlfIIM/index.html.

# Language Focus

## Ⅰ. Useful Expressions

(1) battling            v. 作战;斗争(battle 的现在分词)
(2) bleak               adj. 黯淡的,无希望的
(3) bulk                n. 体积,容量;大多数,大部分;大块
(4) commodity           n. 商品,货物;日用品
(5) enviously           adv. 羡慕地;嫉妒地
(6) mire                n. 泥潭;[地理] 泥沼
(7) ore                 n. 矿;矿石
(8) remarkable          adj. 卓越的;非凡的;值得注意的
(9) replicate           v. 重复;折转
(10) stabilizing        n. 稳定化;稳定化处理

## Ⅱ. Difficult Sentences

(1) The past three months in China have shown what can be achieved if the pandemic is brought under control: China's GDP in the third quarter grew 4.9 percent compared with the previous year, showing that the economy is on a solid track to the pre-pandemic levels.

翻译:中国过去三个月的经历表明,如果疫情得到控制,是可以取得以下成效的:中国第三季度 GDP 同比增长 4.9%,表明中国经济稳步恢复到疫情前的水平。

分析:句子主干为 The past three months have shown what can be achieved。what 引导宾语从句,从句中 if 引导条件状语。showing 及后面的句子是结果状语。

(2) And the supply of masks from China means countries battling against the coronavirus can buy a large bulk of masks and protective suits quickly and at an affordable price.

翻译:中国提供大量的口罩,意味着正在与疫情抗争中的其他各国可以快速、实惠地买到大量口罩和防护服。

分析:该句为省略 that 的宾语从句, the supply of masks from China means countries 后面的 battling against 是现在分词作后置定语,修饰 countries。该句主干为 the supply of masks means countries can buy masks and protective suits。

# Exercises

## Ⅰ. Reading and Understanding

**1. Choose the best answer to each question.**

(1) Which of the following is the recovery path of the economy of China?

A. The closing of all industries

B. Private actions to trace contacts

C. Carryout testing at a large scale

D. All the above

(2) According to the text, which of the following suffered the most from the pandemic?

A. Movie industry

B. Catering businesses

C. Travel agencies

D. None of the above

（3）What is the concern of China's economy?

A. China's growth was mainly driven by imports of medical equipment from other countries.

B. Imports have already resumed to pre-pandemic levels.

C. Imports becomes a stabilizing factor for global industrial and supply chains.

D. The price of masks and protective suites are higher than pre-pandemic levels.

（4）Which of the following is China buying from other countries?

A. Protective suits

B. Masks

C. Respirators

D. Palm oil

（5）What is the author's attitude toward the future of China's economy?

A. Positive

B. Pessimistic

C. Neutral

D. Not mentioned

**2. Decide whether the statements are true or false.**

（1）The first three quarters have witnessed a growth in the farming, industry and services sectors.

（2）There is a strong growth of the world's largest luxury goods company in its China market.

（3）The sales of piazza have grown greatly in China till the end of 2021.

（4）In September, people can afford the price of masks and protective suits.

（5）China is buying more iron ore from Brazil, more soybeans and pork from the U.S., and more palm oil from Malaysia.

**Ⅱ. Translating the Paragraph into English**

世界或许会羡慕中国的经济复苏,但中国的复苏之路却很难被其他国家复制:先彻底关闭相关区域,减少人员流动,然后逐步重新开放所有行业。有一些小规模的 COVID-19 感染病例,但也很快得到控制。政府迅速采取行动追踪接触者,并进行大规模病例检测。

处处是充满希望的迹象。在第二季度中,只有农业经济增长。但是在第三季度中,工业和服务业也开始复苏。这意味着人们有更多的时间消费。在前三季度,网上零售额增长了 15.3%。

## Ⅲ. Developing Critical Thinking

**Work in pairs and discuss the questions.**
(1) How does China handle the health crisis?
(2) Why will China be "the key driver of global growth" in 2020 and 2021?

扫码看答案

# Text B   Country Roads Lead to Success

At the crack of dawn, Peng Chunling can be found busily loading ripe watermelons onto a truck. From growing grains to planting melons in a highly efficient agricultural operation, villagers like Peng of Zhenzhuozhuang Village, Suqian City in Jiangsu Province, have seen their incomes rise and livelihoods flourish. And all the positive changes can be ascribed to one thing—construction and upgrading of rural roads.

## Booming Rural Tourism

Rural roads are a basic requirement for rural economic and social development. In the past, the weak transportation infrastructure was a bottleneck for the development of the Chengzi Lake area in Siyang County, Suqian City. While in recent years, a total of 1 billion RMB has been invested in key transportation projects in this area, improving interconnectivity of the county via expressways and provincial highways with better developed urban areas.

Apart from connecting to outside markets, the upgraded rural roads have also facilitated the development of tourism. Several ecotourism projects have already been completed in the Chengzi Lake Tourist Resort in Siyang County.

As the roads have become more accessible, the surrounding environment has improved. Zhao Yuqin, a resident of the Chengzi River Community, has personally witnessed these developments and changes.

"Houses and sanitation facilities have been built, and the greening project has beautified the roadsides. I can earn money working in a fruit company. Now, my annual income exceeds 20,000 RMB. We are content with our life," said Zhao.

Like Zhao Yuqin, there are many farmers benefiting from the improved transportation. "The roads used to be unpaved and the villages were untidy. Now, the sanitation and the environment have greatly improved thanks to the new roads," said Shao Qizhuang, a senior villager living at the Bohu Residential Community in Siyang County.

At present, the mode of "rural road+tourism" has seen more farmers in Suqian City get rich. Making use of the new rural roads in the Chengzi Lake area, Siyang County government invested nearly 30 million RMB in building a peach park at Luji Township, an agricultural scenic spot which is expected to increase local collective income by nearly 300,000 RMB. In 2019, Suqian City received 27.87 million tourists, who brought a tourism revenue of 33.6 billion RMB. The per capita disposable income of local rural residents has exceeded 18,000 RMB.

## Connected by E-Commerce

How many packages can a delivery center in a Chinese town handle every day? Hu Yun, who manages such a delivery center in Xinhe Town, Shuyang County of Suqian City, offered an answer: around 10,000. "At the peak time, the figure reached 80,000," Hu said, attributing the brisk business to upgraded transportation.

Hu's delivery service center is just one of many in the E-commerce Express Park in Xinhe Town, the first of its kind in Jiangsu Province. Built in 2016 with an investment of 5 million RMB, the park now houses 11 courier services companies.

"From January to July this year, the park has processed and shipped out more than 19 million shipments. It is estimated that the 26 express delivery centers in the park will ship out more than 70 million shipments this year," said Ge Hengping, Party chief of Xinhe Town.

Fueling the buoyant courier services is the bonsai planting business that underpins the township economy.

Xinhe Town is home to 11,000 online stores selling bonsai plants, and the annual sales exceed 2.5 billion RMB. "After the express park started operation, it has provided efficient and convenient delivery services for farmers, effectively promoting a sound development of the bonsai planting industry," said Ge.

At the bonsai market in Zhouquan Village in Xinhe Town, Jiang Aihua is busy trimming and packaging bonsai orders for her customers. At the same time, she is live streaming her daily routine via a social media platform. In one hour, she attracts more than 20,000 online viewers, and receives over 20 orders worth 10,000 RMB. "In the past, we had to send the goods to the downtown market. Since the bonsai is too large to transport, transportation was a problem. Now with the roads built, we can package the goods at home and use the door-to-door delivery service," said Jiang.

Through the rural roads, the courier service in Xinhe Town has become fast and efficient. Today, there is an average of 2.2 parcels sent across the world every second from Xinhe Town.

## Rural Vitalization

Infrastructure connectivity has fueled thriving agricultural industries in Suqian. Since 2014, like Siyang, some other counties including Shuyang and Sihong in Suqian have also witnessed rapid growth of industries suitable to local conditions.

Farmers in Dianhu Village, Sihong County, have long been growing pecan seedlings. In 2014, a pecan seedlings nursery measuring about 2.7 hectares was built. Local farmers' concern at the time was how to ship the seedlings out of the remote hinterland village.

They were emboldened to expand the nursery business a year later as a highway connecting Suqian with Nanjing, capital of Jiangsu Province, and neighboring Shanghai region, was completed.

Today, the formerly poor Dianhu Village takes on a totally different look featuring broad roads, rows of new houses, and stretches of greenhouses, along with more than 10 companies that have settled there. He Xiaojiao, a local firm's employee, said, "Now we can find a job without leaving the village. Our annual income can reach 40,000 to 50,000 RMB."

Transportation connectivity is also a priority of local governments in fighting poverty. Since 2012, Suqian City has invested 1.5 billion RMB to develop transport infrastructure, which has uplifted nearly 100,000 people out of poverty. "The transportation now available for bringing in supplies and selling our grain has made business much more convenient than before. It saves labor and expense. I contracted out 220 hectares of land, which now generates an annual net income of 800,000 RMB or more for my family," said Shi Suwen, a major grain farmer working in the area.

In Henan Village of Sihong County, the decrepit village road was only 3.5 meters in width. Now it has been renovated and broadened out to 5.5 meters. "It connects our farmland and has brought tangible benefits to our farmers," said Zhu Xiumin, Party chief of Henan Village, noting that the 3.2-km-long broad road makes people's daily life much easier.

"In the past, due to poor road conditions, when it snowed or rained, we had to stop business; now transport is no longer a concern. In the past, we traveled on foot or by bicycle; now every household has motorcycles or even cars. In the past, we farmers went on a long journey to see urban scenery; now urbanites come to enjoy the idyllic rural life," said Ge Yimei, a farmer from Qiaozhuang Village in Sihong.

Coming along with the improved road conditions is a rising number of tourists and returning of young people starting up businesses in their hometowns, according to Ge Yimei, who believes the youth is the future of the countryside.

As rural roads are spreading all over the country and helping accelerate rural vitalization, China's hinterland villages are becoming more prosperous, modern, and livable.

**Source**:

http://www.chinatoday.com.cn/ctenglish/2018/et/202011/t20201127_800228319.html.

## Language Focus

### Ⅰ. Useful Expressions

| | |
|---|---|
| (1) be ascribed to | 归结于 |
| (2) bonsai | *n.* 盆景;盆景艺术 |
| (3) buoyant courier services | 活跃的快递服务 |
| (4) decrepit | *adj.* 衰老的;破旧的 |
| (5) embolden | *v.* (使)有胆量,更勇敢;鼓励;(使)有信心 |
| (6) facilitated | *v.* 促进;帮助(facilitate 的过去分词);使有利于发展 |
| (7) infrastructure | *n.* 基础设施;公共建设;下部构造 |
| (8) renovated | *v.* 更新,革新;修复;重新布置(renovate 的过去式) |

(9) sanitation　　　　　　　　n. [医]环境卫生;卫生设备;下水道设施
(10) shipments　　　　　　　n. 发货;运载的货物(shipment 的复数)
(11) tangible　　　　　　　　adj. 有形的;切实的;可触摸的
(12) thriving　　　　　　　　adj. 欣欣向荣的,兴旺发达的
(13) trim　　　　　　　　　　v. 修剪;切除(不规则或不需要的部分)
(14) underpins　　　　　　　v. 巩固;支持;从下面支撑;加强……的基础
(15) vitalization　　　　　　　n. 赋予生命

## Ⅱ. Difficult Sentences

(1) While in recent years, a total of 1 billion RMB has been invested in key transportation projects in this area, improving interconnectivity of the county via expressways and provincial highways with better developed urban areas.

**翻译**:近年来,总共有10亿元人民币投入到该地区的重点交通项目中,通过高速公路和省道加强了县城与较发达城市地区的互联互通。

**分析**:improving 是现在分词作状语,表示目的。该句主干为 a total of 1 billion RMB has been invested in key transportation projects。

(2) Making use of the new rural roads in the Chengzi Lake area, Siyang County government invested nearly 30 million RMB in building a peach park at Luji Township, an agricultural scenic spot which is expected to increase local collective income by nearly 300,000 RMB.

**翻译**:泗阳县政府利用城子湖地区新农村公路,投资近3000万元,在鲁集乡建设了一个桃园农业景区,预期将使当地集体收入增加近30万元。

**分析**:Making use the new rural roads in the Chengzi Lake area 是现在分词作方式状语。which is expected to increase local collective income by nearly 300,000 RMB 为定语从句,修饰先行词 an agricultural scenic spot。该句主干为 Siyang County government invested nearly 30 million RMB in building a peach park。

(3) Coming along with the improved road conditions is a rising number of tourists and returning of young people starting up businesses in their hometowns, according to Ge Yimei, who believes the youth is the future of the countryside.

翻译:葛一美认为,随着路况的改善,越来越多的游客来到这里,也有越来越多的年轻人回到家乡创业。她认为年轻人是农村的未来。

分析:Coming along with the improved road conditions 是动名词作主语。starting up businesses in their hometowns 为现在分词作后置定语。句子主干为 Coming along with the improved road conditions is a rising number of tourists and returning of young people。

# Exercises

## Ⅰ. Reading and Understanding

**Answer the following questions.**

(1) What are basic requirements for rural economic and social development?

(2) What does Xinhe Town do for its living?

(3) What is/are the priority/ies of local governments in fighting poverty?

(4) How many people are at least interviewed to finish the report?

(5) What changes toward people's life does the road building bring?

## Ⅱ. Dealing with Unfamiliar Words

**Choose the word that best fits in the blank.**

(1) In this period, there were 974 outbreaks of communicable disease _____ to the consumption of raw milk.

A. attribute

B. ascribe

C. prescribe

D. due

(2) The report is _____ by extensive research.

A. underpinned

B. support

C. written

D. conducted

(3) None the less, in a just and _____ economy, an effective criminal justice system has important functions to perform.

A. prospers

B. thriving

C. flourish

D. bombing

(4) Past the overgrown lawn, through the _____ rose arbour and into the wilderness.

A. descriptive

B. creepy

C. decrepit

D. old

(5) Now the buildings are being _____ into 41 apartments, mainly for families earning less than $30,000 a year.

A. innovated

B. renovated

C. repair

D. restore

## Ⅲ. Translating the Paragraph into English

在新河镇周泉村的盆景市场,蒋爱华正忙着为顾客修剪、包装盆景订单。同时,她还通过社交媒体平台直播自己的日常生活。在一个小时内,她吸引了两万多名在线观众,收到了20多个订单,价值一万元人民币。"过去,我们得把货送到市中心市场。由于盆景太大,无法运输,运输成了一个问题。现在道路建成后,我们可以在家里包装货物,并使用送货上门服务。"蒋爱华说。

## Ⅳ. Developing Critical Thinking

**Work in pairs and discuss the questions.**

(1) Since according to the passage, China's hinterland villages are becoming more prosperous, modern, and livable. What do you think will happen to rural migrant workers in the future? Will it affect the development of cities then?

(2) Apart from what are described in the passage, can you think of any other means to promote rural economic development?

扫码看答案

# 参考文献
## References

[1] 江进林,韩宝成.基于Coh-Metrix的大学英语六级与托福、雅思阅读语篇难度研究[J].中国外语,2018(3):86-95.

[2] 李秀英,寇金南,关晓薇,等.新时代大学英语课程思政:"明德"与"思辨"——以《新时代明德大学英语综合教程3》为例[J].中国外语,2021,18(2):39-46.

[3] 刘正光,钟玲俐,任远.落实新《指南》,对接"立德树人"新需求——"新目标大学英语"《综合教程》修订的理念与特色[J].外语界,2021(2):25-30.

[4] 马文丽.中国当代英文报话语分析[M].北京:中央编译出版社,2011.

[5] Simon Greenhall,文秋芳.新标准大学英语综合教程2[M].2版.北京:外语教学与研究出版社,2016.

[6] 孙有中,侯毅凌.大学思辨英语教程精读2:文学与人生[M].北京:外语教学与研究出版社,2016.

[7] 杨桂华,赵智云.培养跨文化能力的大学英语阅读教学实践研究[J].外语界,2018(3):26-31.

[8] 张敬源,王娜,曹红晖.大学英语新形态一体化教材建设探索与实践——兼析《通用学术英语》的编写理念与特色[J].中国外语,2017,14(2):81-85.

[9] 张晓艺.英语阅读能力描述语的"可理解性"研究:外语学习者视角[J].外语界,2017(5):12-21.

[10] 赵雯,王海啸.新时代大学英语语言能力的建构[J].外语界,2020(4):19-27.

## 与本书配套的数字资源使用说明

　　本书部分课程及与纸质教材配套的数字资源以二维码链接的形式呈现。使用手机微信扫码成功后提示微信登录，授权后进入注册页面，填写注册信息。按照提示输入手机号码，点击获取手机验证码，稍等片刻，可收到4位数的验证码短信，在提示位置输入验证码成功，再设置密码，选择相应专业，点击"立即注册"，即注册成功。（若手机已经注册，则在"注册"页面底部选择"已有账号？立即登录"，进入"账号绑定"页面，直接输入手机号和密码登录。）接着按提示输入学习码，需刮开教材封面防伪涂层，输入13位学习码（正版图书拥有的一次性使用学习码），输入正确后提示绑定成功，即可查看数字数字资源。手机第一次登录查看资源成功以后，再次使用数字资源时，只需在微信端扫码即可登录进入查看。